BEYOND
COMMODITIES

BEYOND COMMODITIES

The Growth Challenge of Latin America and the Caribbean

Jorge Thompson Araujo, Ekaterina Vostroknutova,
Markus Brueckner, Mateo Clavijo, and
Konstantin M. Wacker

 **WORLD BANK GROUP**

Latin American Development Forum Series

This series was created in 2003 to promote debate, disseminate information and analysis, and convey the excitement and complexity of the most topical issues in economic and social development in Latin America and the Caribbean. It is sponsored by the Inter-American Development Bank, the United Nations Economic Commission for Latin America and the Caribbean, and the World Bank, and represents the highest quality in each institution's research and activity output. Titles in the series have been selected for their relevance to the academic community, policy makers, researchers, and interested readers, and have been subjected to rigorous anonymous peer review prior to publication.

Advisory Committee Members

Alicia Bárcena Ibarra, Executive Secretary, Economic Commission for Latin America and the Caribbean, United Nations

Inés Bustillo, Director, Washington Office, Economic Commission for Latin America and the Caribbean, United Nations

Augusto de la Torre, Chief Economist, Latin America and the Caribbean Region, World Bank

Daniel Lederman, Deputy Chief Economist, Latin America and the Caribbean Region, World Bank

Santiago Levy, Vice President for Sectors and Knowledge, Inter-American Development Bank

Roberto Rigobon, Professor of Applied Economics, MIT Sloan School of Management

José Juan Ruiz, Chief Economist and Manager of the Research Department, Inter-American Development Bank

Ernesto Talvi, Director, Brookings Global-CERES Economic and Social Policy in Latin America Initiative

Andrés Velasco, Cieplan, Chile

Titles in the Latin American Development Forum Series

Discrimination in Latin America: An Economic Perspective (2010) by Hugo Ñopo, Alberto Chong, and Andrea Moro, editors

The Promise of Early Childhood Development in Latin America and the Caribbean (2010) by Emiliana Vegas and Lucrecia Santibáñez

Job Creation in Latin America and the Caribbean: Trends and Policy Challenges (2009) by Carmen Pagés, Gaëlle Pierre, and Stefano Scarpetta

China's and India's Challenge to Latin America: Opportunity or Threat? (2009) by Daniel Lederman, Marcelo Olarreaga, and Guillermo E. Perry, editors

Does the Investment Climate Matter? Microeconomic Foundations of Growth in Latin America (2009) by Pablo Fajnzylber, Jose Luis Guasch, and J. Humberto López, editors

Measuring Inequality of Opportunities in Latin America and the Caribbean (2009) by Ricardo de Paes Barros, Francisco H. G. Ferreira, José R. Molinas Vega, and Jaime Saavedra Chanduvi

The Impact of Private Sector Participation in Infrastructure: Lights, Shadows, and the Road Ahead (2008) by Luis Andres, Jose Luis Guasch, Thomas Haven, and Vivien Foster

Remittances and Development: Lessons from Latin America (2008) by Pablo Fajnzylber and J. Humberto López, editors

Fiscal Policy, Stabilization, and Growth: Prudence or Abstinence? (2007) by Guillermo Perry, Luis Servén, and Rodrigo Suescún, editors

Raising Student Learning in Latin America: Challenges for the 21ˢᵗ Century (2007) by Emiliana Vegas and Jenny Petrow

Investor Protection and Corporate Governance: Firm-Level Evidence Across Latin America (2007) by Alberto Chong and Florencio López-de-Silanes, editors

Natural Resources: Neither Curse nor Destiny (2007) by Daniel Lederman and William F. Maloney, editors

The State of State Reform in Latin America (2006) by Eduardo Lora, editor

Emerging Capital Markets and Globalization: The Latin American Experience (2006) by Augusto de la Torre and Sergio L. Schmukler

Beyond Survival: Protecting Households from Health Shocks in Latin America (2006) by Cristian C. Baeza and Truman G. Packard

Beyond Reforms: Structural Dynamics and Macroeconomic Vulnerability (2005) by José Antonio Ocampo, editor

Privatization in Latin America: Myths and Reality (2005) by Alberto Chong and Florencio López-de-Silanes, editors

Keeping the Promise of Social Security in Latin America (2004) by Indermit S. Gill, Truman G. Packard, and Juan Yermo

Lessons from NAFTA: For Latin America and the Caribbean (2004) by Daniel Lederman, William F. Maloney, and Luis Servén

The Limits of Stabilization: Infrastructure, Public Deficits, and Growth in Latin America (2003) by William Easterly and Luis Servén, editors

Globalization and Development: A Latin American and Caribbean Perspective (2003) by José Antonio Ocampo and Juan Martin, editors

Is Geography Destiny? Lessons from Latin America (2003) by John Luke Gallup, Alejandro Gaviria, and Eduardo Lora

Contents

Boxes

Figures

Tables

Executive Summary

The Latin America and the Caribbean (LAC) region has had a "decade of convergence." During the past decade, countries in LAC exhibited high growth rates and recovered quickly after the global financial crisis. The region benefited from favorable external conditions, in particular high commodity prices, and relatively loose financial conditions, especially in the United States. LAC lost considerable ground vis-à-vis U.S. income levels from 1980 until the early 2000s, but has converged somewhat to the U.S. level since then. The rate of growth in LAC has been higher in this period, but also higher than the rate in the United States (and many advanced economies), hence constituting a "decade of convergence."

The recent growth performance in LAC has been especially pro-poor. Not only the overall pattern of growth has changed, but also by and large growth has been more favorable to the bottom 40 percent. The incomes of the bottom 40 percent have been growing faster than average income in LAC countries over this period, and growth seems to have become more pro-poor in the post-2000 period.

Understanding the factors underlying LAC's growth performance is critical for policy design going forward. Facing future demographic challenges and a likely "new normal" environment, where the commodity super cycle has come to an end and external financing conditions turn less favorable, it is important to understand the factors underlying growth in LAC in the recent period. Was LAC significantly different from other regions? Did the determinants of growth in LAC change significantly over the past decade? What role did external conditions play in this context?

This study reassesses LAC's engines of growth in light of new data and information. External conditions and policy decisions in the 2000s to a large extent favored the region. However, the region's "good fortune" seems to be running out, and the determinants of growth that are influenced by policy will play a larger role if the region wants to avoid losing its growth momentum. This study draws on and extends the literature on cross-country regressions as the main empirical strategy to identify the determinants of growth. The study builds on the econometric approach of Loayza,

Fajnzylber, and Calderón (2005), with some important extensions. Using dynamic panel data regressions, this approach investigates how aggregate economic, political, and social variables affect growth rates of per capita gross domestic product (GDP) for a large sample of countries. To distinguish the impact of policy reforms from the commodity boom in the past decade, the study uses a country-specific commodity export price index, which captures windfalls arising from booms in international commodity prices.

A main finding of the study is that drivers of growth in LAC shifted over the past decade. Compared with previous studies on the subject (for example, Loayza, Fajnzylber, and Calderón 2005), this study finds less evidence of the role of stabilization-related variables for growth in LAC. This finding potentially reflects that most countries in LAC had their macroeconomic house in order throughout the 1990s, which facilitated their ability to reap the benefits of other sources of growth in the period thereafter, but did not constitute a means of growth. Conversely, structural features continued to play a key role in growth. But for many countries in LAC, most notably net commodity exporters, external conditions were an essential driver of growth over the past decade. This broad pattern suggests that some sources of growth can shift over time. External conditions might change in the future and are mostly beyond the region's control. Structural features are easier to shape and have turned out as a robust determinant of growth.

Within LAC, however, there is a great deal of heterogeneity across countries and in-country changes over time. The heterogeneity across countries is noteworthy, for example, by the contrast between Haiti and Panama in growth performance. The heterogeneity in in-country changes over time is shown by the instructive example of Chile. Loayza, Fajnzylber, and Calderón (2005) find that Chile's growth was explained mostly by structural reforms. However, the most important factor in explaining the country's recent growth performance seems to be external conditions. This does not mean that Chile's structural reform process stagnated or reversed, but only that its contribution to growth became less relevant than that of external conditions. Combined with the widespread adoption of structural reform initiatives across the region, the commodity boom also facilitated the emergence of new "growth stars" in LAC. There is now a larger set of faster growing countries in LAC than at the time of the study by Loayza, Fajnzylber, and Calderón (2005), because of external conditions and structural reforms. Chile is joined by countries such as Colombia, the Dominican Republic, Panama, and Peru as fast-growing LAC economies.

This study carried out a benchmarking exercise that sheds light on where the "biggest bang for the buck" could be for countries in LAC, without attempting to identify the ultimate sources of growth. This exercise looks into the counterfactual per capita income a country would have achieved if it were a top performer for each explanatory variable. The findings help to determine the possible effects that a stellar performance (relative to the rest of LAC) in specific policy-sensitive areas might have had for a country's level of GDP per capita. Better performance in stabilization-related features of the economy clearly would have benefited Argentina, Ecuador, and República Bolivariana de Venezuela, while having a significantly lower impact elsewhere in the region. The counterfactual impact of improved structural features varies widely across the region, where the main would-be beneficiaries of improvements in various structural factors include Guatemala (education), Nicaragua (infrastructure), and República Bolivariana de Venezuela (financial development).

The empirical findings provide a window into the potential growth-facilitating role of governments in the region. On the one hand, government consumption would have a negative impact on growth—after controlling for macroeconomic stability and structural features such as national security as well as law and order—to the extent that it represents a proxy for government *burden*. That is, government consumption potentially implies distortions (such as high taxes) or inefficiencies (such as a bloated public bureaucracy), without generating clear social returns. On the other hand, education and infrastructure services—which are at least partly funded by the public sector—would have a positive impact on growth. Therefore, *the composition of public spending matters for growth*. The impact of public spending will be positive only if it helps support the accumulation of human capital (through education) or physical capital (through infrastructure). More broadly, governments can also facilitate growth by maintaining a stable and predictable policy environment, at the macro- and microeconomic levels.

Acknowledgments

This report was co authored by Jorge Thompson Araujo (Economic Adviser, LCRVP), Ekaterina Vostroknutova (Lead Economist, GMFDR), Konstantin Wacker (Assistant Professor of International Economics, Gutenberg University, Mainz), Markus Brueckner (Professor of Economics, National University, Singapore), and Mateo Clavijo (Financial Analyst, GFMDR), as part of the Regional Studies Program of the Office of the Regional Chief Economist, Latin America and the Caribbean Vice-Presidency. The authors thank Augusto de la Torre (Chief Economist, LCRCE), Auguste Kouame (Practice Manager, GMFDR), and Daniel Lederman (Deputy Chief Economist, LCRCE) for very effective guidance and support throughout, as well as the peer reviewers Pedro Cavalcanti Ferreira (Professor of Economics, Fundação Getúlio Vargas, Rio de Janeiro, Brazil), Gerardo Esquivel (Professor of Economics, Colégio de México), and César Calderón (Lead Economist, AFRCE) for the excellent comments provided during the concept and decision stages of preparation of this report. Very helpful comments from John Panzer (Director, GMFDR), Norman Loayza (Lead Economist, DECMG), Francesco Caselli (Professor of Economics, London School of Economics), and Jaime de Piniés (Lead Economist, GMFO5) are gratefully acknowledged. Helpful comments from two anonymous referees are also gratefully acknowledged. Thanks are also due to Matias Antonio (Junior Professional Associate, GMFDR) for revamping the benchmarking tool derived from the empirical analysis in this report, as well as to Miriam Villarroel (Program Assistant, GMFDR), Silvia Gulino (Program Assistant, GMFDR), and Diana Lachy (Program Assistant, GMFDR) for excellent assistance throughout the preparation of this report.

About the Authors

Jorge Thompson Araujo is an economic adviser in the Office of the Vice President, Latin America and the Caribbean. Mr. Araujo joined the World Bank in 1996 as an economist. He has since held various positions in the Middle East and North Africa, Sub-Saharan Africa, and Latin America and the Caribbean regions, as well as corporate assignments in the organization. Before joining the Work Bank, he was an associate professor of economics at the University of Brasilia, Brazil. Mr. Araujo has published widely in the areas of economic growth, functional distribution of income, and public finance. He co-authored the recent World Bank regional report, *Understanding the Income and Efficiency Gap in Latin America and the Caribbean* in the Directions in Development series. He holds a PhD in economics from the University of Cambridge, United Kingdom, and an M.Sc. in Eeonomics from the University of Brasilia.

Ekaterina Vostroknutova is a lead economist in the World Bank's Eastern Europe and Central Asia Region. Ms. Vostroknutova joined the World Bank in 2003 as a Young Professional in the core team of the World Development Report and has since been in various positions in the East Asia and Pacific and Latin America and the Caribbean regions. She holds a PhD in economics from the European University Institute, a degree in applied mathematics from Moscow State University, and a master's degree in economics from the European University at St. Petersburg. Ms. Vostroknutova's fields of interest include microeconomic foundations of economic growth and fiscal and monetary policy.

Markus Brueckner is a professor in the Research School of Economics of the Australian National University. Previous appointments include a Professorship at the University of Queensland during 2014–2015; an appointment as associate professor at the National University of Singapore during 2011–2014; and senior lecturer at the University of Adelaide during 2010–2011. His main teaching and research interests are in the field of economic growth and development. He has published widely in leading international journals and is regularly a referee in the peer-review process of these journals. His research has been featured in *Bloomberg, Financial Times, The New York Times, The Wall Street Journal,* and *The Economist.* Professor Brueckner has been engaged in numerous consulting projects for the International Monetary Fund and the World Bank. He earned a PhD in economics from the Universitat Pompeu Fabra in Spain in 2010. He previously received a BA in economics from the University of Mannheim in 2006.

Mateo Clavijo is a financial analyst in the World Banks's Finance and Markets Global Practice for the Latin American region. Mr. Clavijo joined the World Bank in 2012 as a Junior Professional Associate at the Macroeconomics and Fiscal Management Unit where he worked on growth and country risk assessments in Latin America. He has also worked as a consultant for the International Finance Corporation and in the private sector in Colombia. His research has focused on cross-country income differences and the effects of financial system imbalances on economic cycles. He holds an M.Sc. in economics and finance from Universitat Pompeu Fabra in Spain and MA and BA degrees in economics from the Universidad de los Andes in Bogotá-Colombia.

Konstantin M. Wacker is an assistant professor at the Gutenberg University of Mainz in Germany. He holds a PhD in economics and applied statistics from the University of Göttingen and has studied in Vienna, Alicante, and Beijing. He previously worked for the World Bank, the European Central Bank, the International Monetary Fund, the United Nations University World Institute for Development Economics Research, and the Lower Austrian Chamber of Labor.

Abbreviations

ComPI	international commodity export price index
CPI	consumer price index
GDP	gross domestic product
GMM	general method of moments
LAC	Latin America and the Caribbean
PPP	purchasing power parity
PWT	Penn World Table
TFP	total factor productivity

1
Introduction

Why This Study?

The Latin America and the Caribbean (LAC) region has achieved a decade of remarkable growth and income convergence. As figure 1.1 illustrates, growth in the LAC region picked up in the early 2000s and reached rates considerably above those in earlier decades, notwithstanding the global financial crisis and subsequent economic depression. For the first time since the early 1980s, there has been a sustained convergence to high-income levels, that is, a higher growth rate than in high-income economies.

Growth has been a key driver for reducing poverty and boosting shared prosperity. As shown in figure 1.2, growth has helped to reduce poverty and raise the income levels of low-income households across countries in LAC. The figure depicts the relationship between growth in average income (horizontal axis) and growth in income of the poorest two quintiles (the bottom 40 percent of each country, vertical axis) for countries in LAC (using data since 1981). The figure shows that, on average, there is nearly a one-to-one relationship between the income growth of the bottom 40 percent and the headline growth rate. Understanding and achieving sustained growth is thus essential for reaching the World Bank's twin goals of eradicating poverty and promoting shared prosperity in general.[1] The most recent growth episode in the region might be of particular interest, as figure 1.3 suggests that the poverty-reducing effect of growth has increased since 2000.

It has been debated how much the decade of growth was driven by policy reforms and how much by favorable external conditions. LAC's remarkable growth performance took place amid a largely supportive external environment. Commodity prices soared, implying terms of trade improvements for the region's commodity exporters, and international borrowing costs were quite low, because there was abundant international liquidity. Apart from the countries that rely heavily on U.S. tourist arrivals, most countries in LAC were relatively shielded from the financial crisis. Some commentators thus argue that LAC's recent growth performance was mostly driven

FIGURE 1.1: Growth in LAC, 1985–2013

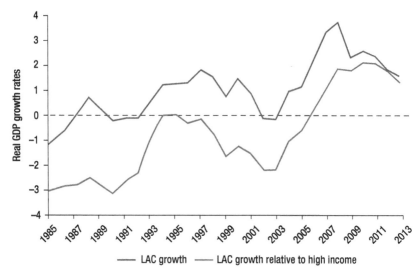

Source: World Bank Group staff calculations based on World Development Indicators data.
Note: Data are five-year moving averages.

FIGURE 1.2: Growth and Incomes of the Poor since 1981

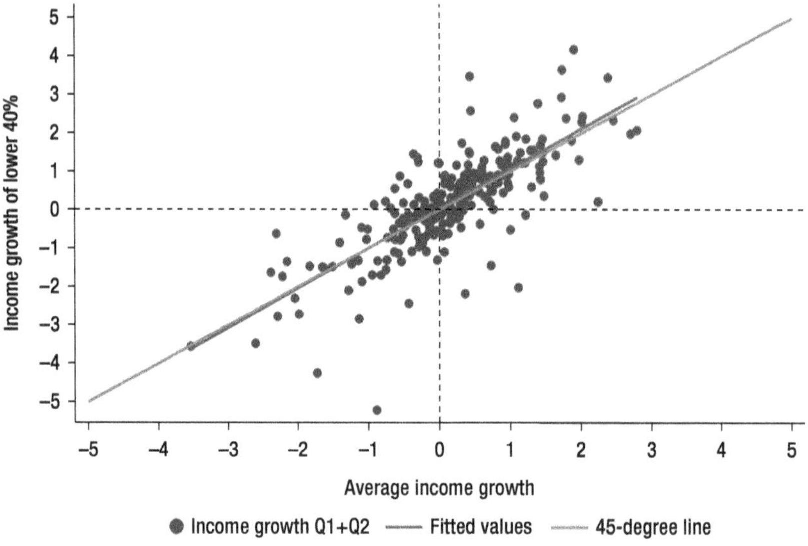

Source: World Bank calculations based on the Dollar, Kleineberg, and Kraay 2016 data set.
Note: The figure includes all household surveys available in LAC countries since 1981.

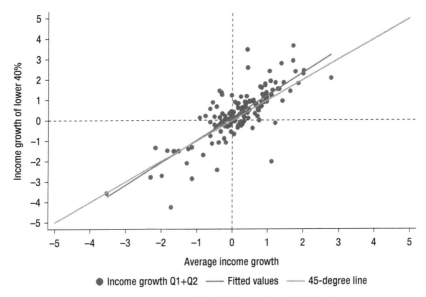

Source: World Bank Group staff calculations based on the Dollar, Kleineberg, and Kraay 2016 data set.
Note: The figure includes all household surveys available in LAC countries since 2000.

by external factors.[2] However, it is also true that many countries in LAC have substantially improved their macroeconomic frameworks over the past two decades. And many have pursued several structural reforms, ranging from improvements in infrastructure to social safety nets, to broad-based education fostering human capital development, which is expected to generate economic growth. This study assesses the relative magnitudes of the effects of the two broad factors—policy reforms and favorable external conditions—on the decade of growth in LAC.

Key Results

Although external factors were supportive and relevant, the effects of domestic policies are just as relevant for explaining LAC's recent growth performance. As our empirical analysis reveals, terms of trade and commodity price improvements have contributed significantly to growth in the LAC region. They contributed about 5 percentage points to the improvement in income over the decade from the late 1990s to the late 2000s. These effects were just as important as the effects of structural policies, which, inter alia, improved human capital and infrastructure.

The emphasis of domestic policy has shifted from stabilization policies to structural policies. Stabilization policies (such as contained inflation) were supportive for the growth effects to materialize. A novel finding over previous analyses of economic growth in the region (such as Loayza, Fajnzylber, and Calderón 2005) is that the growth effects of incremental improvements in this dimension over the past decade were limited. Although it will be important to maintain macroeconomic stability in the future—especially in the context of a complex global macroeconomic environment—further structural reforms will be key to sustain growth and income convergence amid a fading commodity price boom.

There is heterogeneity across countries in LAC in the key drivers of growth. Although the individual effects of the determinants of growth do not vary significantly across countries, the countries experienced different developments in those variables. For example, while commodity prices were supportive, several net commodity importers saw remarkable growth as well, caused by improvements in structural policies. This heterogeneity reflects the equally important relevance of external conditions and domestic policies.

In addition, the benchmarking exercise in this study reveals which policy gaps will lead to the highest potential growth payoffs for each country, and helps identify potential trade-offs. The analysis applies the results from the econometric growth exercise to existing gaps in key variables across countries in LAC, to estimate how countries could sustain growth most promisingly into the future. For example, some countries could still see high growth effects from improving their macroeconomic stabilization frameworks, while for others—most notably in Central America—structural policy should be a policy priority.

Outline of the Report

The report uses descriptive statistics and growth econometrics to analyze growth in LAC. The report begins by highlighting some stylized facts about the recent growth experience in the region (chapter 2). Chapter 3 presents the econometric framework and data that underlie the report. The model uses panel data for more than 100 countries over 1970–2010 to identify which policies and factors have driven economic growth across countries. The report focuses on several aspects and outcomes of this model, instead of performing a collection of standard, but often superficial, tools to analyze growth.[3] The analysis includes a series of robustness checks to ensure that the model works properly.

The report uses the results of the analysis to explain the pattern of growth in LAC over the past decade, for looking ahead and to identify potential policy gaps. Chapters 4 and 5 discuss the roles of external and domestic policy factors, respectively, based on the econometric results. Several extensions of the basic model, including policy interactions and alternative measures of infrastructure, are examined in chapter 6. Then, in chapter 7, the report considers how growth in the region could potentially look, should past patterns of growth persist into the future. An important contribution of the study is that it is a benchmarking exercise. The report identifies the potential income effects that countries would realize by closing the gap with the top performers in key variables that are found to have an impact on growth and income. Policy implications are discussed in chapter 8, and chapter 9 concludes.

Notes

1. The recent literature has stressed that the relationship between growth and poverty reduction is complex and far from unidirectional. See, for example, Cohen and Easterly (2009) and especially the contributions by Ravallion and Banerjee therein. Recent calculations by Crespo-Cuaresma, Klasen, and Wacker (2016) further suggest that, while making a considerable difference for poverty reduction, growth will not be sufficient on its own for eradicating poverty by 2030.

2. See, for example, Perry (2014, 1): "But the recent slowdown has revealed what a number of analysts insisted on during that era: the boom was fundamentally driven by exogenous factors, first and foremost of which was the commodity prices super cycle that produced continuous increases in our [LAC's] terms of trade (except in 2009)."

3. For example, we do not perform a growth accounting exercise, because, inter alia, such an exercise would suffer from the problem that capital stock cannot respond quickly to economic downturns. However, Caselli (2016), in a background paper to a companion report, provides an in-depth development accounting exercise for the region.

References

Caselli, Francesco. 2016. "The Latin American Efficiency Gap." In *Understanding Latin America and the Caribbean's Income Gap*, edited by J. Araujo, M. Clavijo, E. Vostroknutova, and K. Wacker. Washington, DC: World Bank.

Cohen, Jessica, and William Easterly, eds. 2009. *What Works in Development? Thinking Big and Thinking Small*. Washington, DC: Brookings Institution Press.

Crespo-Cuaresma, Jesús, Stephan Klasen, and Konstantin M. Wacker. 2016. "There *Is* Poverty Convergence." Working Paper 213, Vienna University of Economics and Business, Vienna, Austria.

Dollar, David, Tatjana Kleineberg, and Aart Kraay. 2016. "Growth Still Is Good for the Poor." *European Economic Review* 81 (1): 68–85.

Loayza, Norman, Pablo Fajnzylber, and César Calderón. 2005. *Economic Growth in Latin America and the Caribbean: Stylized Facts, Explanations, and Forecasts*. Washington, DC: World Bank Group.

Perry, G. 2014. "Latin America after the Boom: Lessons and Challenges." Published on Latin America & Caribbean: Opportunities for All. http://blogs.worldbank.org/latinamerica, May 1.

2
Stylized Facts

Overview of Growth in the Region

Throughout the past decade, growth in Latin America and the Caribbean (LAC) generally picked up, and growth patterns shifted across countries. Figure 2.1 compares growth in LAC economies after 2000 (vertical axis) with growth over an equally long period before 2000 (horizontal axis). One broad pattern that emerges from this figure and motivates further exploration is the shift of growth to the left of the 45-degree line for most of the economies, especially large ones.[1] This finding implies that, for many countries in LAC, growth over the post-2000 period was higher than growth before 2000. Several new "growth stars" emerged—countries such as Colombia, Panama, and Peru moved way to the left of the 45-degree line. Other countries, such as Chile and Uruguay, maintained a solid growth performance above 2 percent over both periods, while some smaller Caribbean and Central American economies fell back on this dimension. A final category of countries, including Mexico, Paraguay, and República Bolivariana de Venezuela, remained in the corner of poor growth performance, below 2 percent per year over both periods. This suggests that several factors held these countries back from achieving higher growth. Bolivia and Brazil are also close to this quadrant. Although they managed to improve their macroeconomic frameworks over the past decade, considerable shortcomings are potentially holding back their performance.

Growth in the past is a poor indicator for recent growth performance. Another broad pattern emerging from figure 2.1 is the small correlation pattern in the data, especially when smaller economies are included in the picture. If growth was fully persistent over time or, equivalently, the factors that drive growth showed no variation over time, all countries would lie on the 45-degree line in figure 2.1.[2] However, this is by far not the case: for the sample of all countries in LAC, there is basically no correlation (correlation coefficient = 0.009). Excluding the smallest countries, the correlation is somewhat larger (0.252). In neither case, however, does regressing later growth on previous

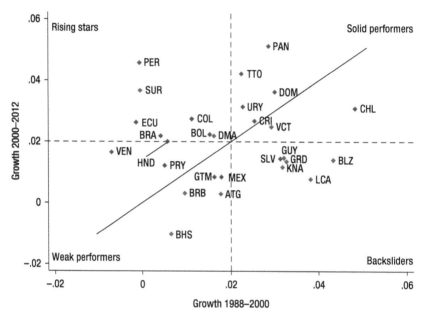

FIGURE 2.1: **Growth of Countries in LAC since 2000 Compared with the Previous Period**

Source: World Bank Group staff calculations; Haver Analytics.
Note: The figure depicts average annual growth in per capita purchasing power parity gross domestic product. ATG = Antigua and Barbuda; BHS = Bahamas; BLZ = Belize; BOL = Bolivia; BRA = Brazil; BRB = Barbados; CHL = Chile; COL = Colombia; CRI = Costa Rica; DMA = Dominica; DOM = Dominican Republic; ECU = Ecuador; GRD = Grenada; GTM = Guatemala; GUY = Guyana; HND = Honduras: KNA = St. Kitts and Nevis; LCA = St. Lucia; MEX = Mexico; PAN = Panama; PER = Peru; PRY = Paraguay; SLV = El Salvador; SUR = Suriname; TTO = Trinidad and Tobago; URY = Uruguay; VCT = St. Vincent and the Grenadines; VEN = República Bolivariana de Venezuela. Caribbean countries are represented by a blue diamond.

growth lead to results that are statistically significant at the 10 percent level.[3] Former growth variation thus explains virtually nothing for later growth variation for the sample of economies in LAC, and only 6 percent for the larger economies in the region.[4]

The increase in growth rates for most economies and the low correlation in growth rates over time raise the question of which factors influenced the variation in growth over time. Were external factors responsible for the observed developments, as many media and policy reports suggest? Or did institutional improvements foster growth? Did the economic relationship between the determinants of growth and growth rates change? Or was there an evolution in the variables explaining growth? These are some of the questions that are addressed in this report.

Not only has there been a change in the overall pattern of growth in LAC, but also growth has been more favorable to the bottom 40 percent. Figure 1.3 (in chapter 1) highlights that the positive relationship between growth and lower-decile income growth is steeper than the 45-degree line for the period after 2000, and thus also steeper than in figure 1.2 (in chapter 1), which takes into account a longer time horizon. This finding means that the incomes of the bottom 40 percent were growing faster than average incomes in countries in LAC over this period, and that growth seems to have become more pro-poor since 2000. This fact is pointed out by Dollar, Kleineberg, and Kraay (2016) and is consistent with Azevedo et al. (2013, tables 7 and 8), who emphasize the role of employment creation as a main factor for poverty reduction in countries in LAC.

Understanding the factors underlying these developments is critical for policy going forward. The region faces future demographic challenges and a likely "new normal" environment, with the commodity super cycle coming to an end and external financing conditions turning less favorable. Thus, it is important to understand the factors that drove growth in LAC in the recent period. Was LAC significantly different from other regions? Did the determinants of growth in LAC change significantly over the past decade? What role did external conditions play in this context?

New data and refined methods allow for improving on earlier studies of growth in the region. The last endeavor to study the drivers of growth in LAC systematically in a comprehensive econometric framework dates back to Loayza, Fajnzylber, and Calderón (2005).[5] Since then, more data have become available that allow for including a decade of new observations in the analysis. Hence, it is possible to investigate whether the economic relationship between the determinants of growth and growth rates themselves changed, or whether the lack of persistence in overall growth rates depicted in figure 2.1 was mainly driven by the fact that there were major changes in the variables that determine economic growth. For example, did stabilization policies become more important for growth, or did LAC advance more on these policies than before? Did external conditions become more relevant for growth in a world that became increasingly globalized, or did the relevance of external conditions remain the same but the conditions themselves became more favorable? The methodology of this report is to estimate the parameters of these determinants using variation over time and internal instruments with the general method of moments. This approach is similar to the methodology of Loayza, Fajnzylber, and Calderón (2005) and various other research, and hence allows for comparison of the results with previous work. Despite the broad methodological similarities, however, progress has been made in the interpretation and evaluation of these models.

Patterns of Growth in LAC

LAC as a whole has seen a decade of convergence. From a wider historical perspective, average income levels in LAC hovered around 20 to 30 percent of the U.S. income level in the past century. Convergence to the income level in most high-income countries, as predicted by standard economic growth models and observed in many Asian economies, has not been achieved by economies in LAC in general. Figure 2.2 depicts the gross domestic product (GDP) of several regions relative to that of the United States. The figure shows that between 1980 and the early 2000s, LAC lost considerable ground vis-à-vis U.S. income levels, but the region converged somewhat to the U.S. level after the early 2000s. Growth in LAC was thus not only higher in this period than before (see figure 2.1), but also higher than growth in the United States (and many high-income economies), hence constituting a decade of convergence.

Figure 2.3 shows that growth has been distributed unevenly across the economies in the region. Countries such as Panama (5.1 percent per year), Peru (4.6 percent), Trinidad and Tobago (4.2 percent), Suriname (3.7 percent), the Dominican Republic (3.6 percent), Uruguay (3.1 percent), and Chile (3.1 percent) all saw average growth rates above 3 percent over the past decade. However, some economies stagnated or even declined, mainly small Caribbean economies, but the region's second largest economy—Mexico—had rather modest growth performance as well (0.8 percent).

FIGURE 2.2: **Regional Income Levels Relative to Income in the United States, 1980–2012**

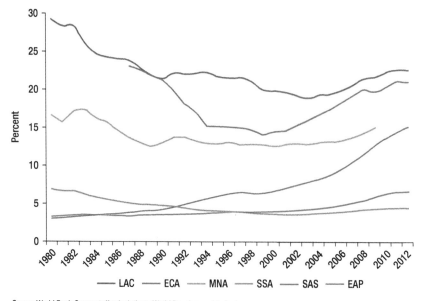

Source: World Bank Group staff calculations; World Development Indicators.
Note: The data show average regional per capita purchasing power parity gross domestic product relative to that of the United States. EAP = East Asia and Pacific; ECA = Europe and Central Asia; LAC = Latin America and the Caribbean; MNA = Middle East and North Africa; SAS = South Asia; SSA = Sub-Saharan Africa.

Growth Rates, 2000–12 (Average Annual Per Capita Growth, Purchasing Power Parity)

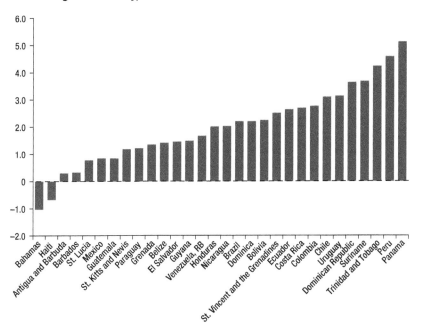

Source: World Bank calculations; World Development Indicators.

A careful look is needed to understand the heterogeneity of growth in the region; no single, simple story can provide a convincing explanation. Although commodity exporters clearly benefitted from favorable terms of trade, this does not explain the strong performance of countries such as Costa Rica or St. Vincent and the Grenadines, or the modest performance of Guyana, Paraguay, or República Bolivariana de Venezuela. Trade openness and more sophisticated macroeconomic frameworks, especially contained inflation rates, are the usual suspects that could have added to growth. However, this argument fails to explain why many Caribbean economies that are open to trade and held inflation in check were stagnating, while countries with more heterodox macroeconomic approaches and periods of relatively high inflation, such as Bolivia and Ecuador, achieved at least satisfactory growth rates. It is thus difficult to distill a clear pattern of growth rates across LAC country groups over the post-2000 period.

It is tempting to attribute causality to single and simple factors that might each influence the region's growth performance; but without a more detailed analysis, such an approach would likely fail to capture adequately the diverse growth experiences in the region. This difficulty raises the familiar question about the determinants of economic growth. Moreover, it requires distinguishing factors that boost growth in the short run but have no sustainable effect on income (such as temporary demand or price effects) from fundamentals that have a long-lasting impact on growth (such as changes in the institutional environment and structural improvements in productivity).

Nonetheless, growth is less heterogeneous across the region today than it was before the 1990s. Figure 2.4 depicts two measures of the heterogeneity of growth across countries in the region over time: the standard deviation and the interquartile range. The figure shows that from 1990 onward, LAC experienced a decline in the heterogeneity of growth. The decrease in the dispersion of growth is especially remarkable considering that growth picked up in the 1990s and especially the 2000s (as illustrated by the red bars in figure 2.3). Usually, it would be expected that an increase in growth would lead to an increase in dispersion measures. Conversely, figure 2.4 suggests that LAC is "growing together," not necessarily in absolute income levels but in growth rates. This finding might reflect convergence in the institutional framework, but also higher reliance on exogenous factors amid fewer policy idiosyncrasies. Looking at simple cross-country correlation coefficients of cyclical growth rates (derived after HP-filtering; see, for example, Sosa 2010 or Böwe and Guillemineau 2006), the findings show that especially open economies in LAC co-move with the

FIGURE 2.4: **Variation in Growth across LAC**

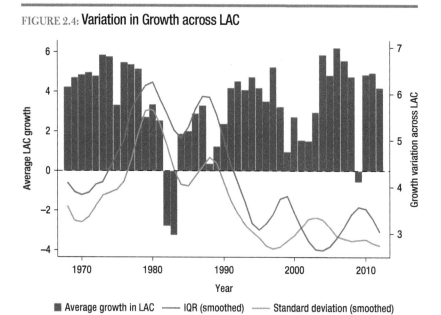

■ Average growth in LAC —— IQR (smoothed) —— Standard deviation (smoothed)

Source: World Bank Group staff calculations based on World Development Indicators data.
Note: IQR = interquartile range.

region in growth. Chile and Mexico show high cyclical correlations with the rest of the larger economies in the region. The strongest pairwise cyclical correlations are found for Chile and Colombia (0.73) and Chile and Mexico (0.71).

Figure 2.5 shows that the contribution of net exports to growth was mostly negative over 2000–11, despite the boom in commodity export prices. The relevant contribution of household consumption and its pro-cyclicality during growth times suggest that growth remained driven by consumption to a considerable degree. Eased credit constraints because of increased commodity revenues and loose global financial conditions might have fueled this development. The negative correlation of net exports with household consumption and investment further suggests that a considerable fraction of domestic demand was satisfied by imports, pointing to potential domestic bottlenecks or frictions in adjustment.

Increased labor force participation was a supportive supply factor, but can only explain part of the growth performance. On the supply side, increases in the labor force participation rate of 0.4 percent per year since 2000 supported the growth of income per capita (figure 2.6). This development was mostly driven by female participation

FIGURE 2.5: Contribution of Expenditure Components to Real GDP Growth in LAC

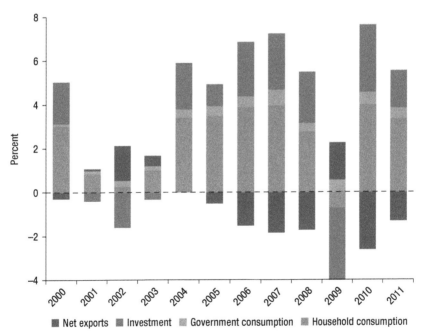

Net exports   Investment   Government consumption   Household consumption

Source: World Bank Group staff calculations based on UNCTAD Stats.
Note: GDP = gross domestic product.

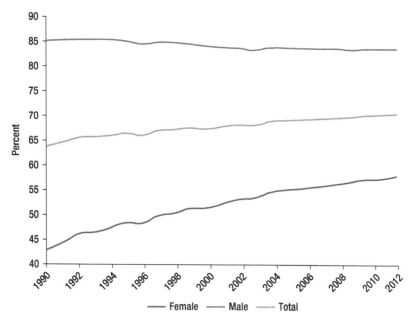

Source: World Bank Group staff calculations; World Development Indicators.

rates (+1 percent per year); male participation rates were essentially flat. Demographic developments also helped, as the ratio of the young and elderly to the working-age population (ages 15–64 years), the so-called age dependency ratio, declined over the past decade. Although higher labor input per capita played a role in growth, the rise in the labor force participation rate was not stronger than in the 1990s, but even some-what slower, so it cannot per se explain the pickup in growth rates.

Furthermore, the countries with the highest increases in labor force participation included not only the top performers in growth (such as Chile, Costa Rica, Peru, and Trinidad and Tobago), but also some that grew moderately (Guatemala) or even shrank (The Bahamas). The country with the highest acceleration in labor force par-ticipation rates in the 2000s compared with the 1990s, Suriname (from −1.1 to 0.5 percent per year), saw an increase in GDP growth rates, but so did the countries with the strongest deceleration in labor force participation, Colombia (from 1.9 to 0.4) and Honduras (from 1.0 to −0.4). These findings indicate that increased labor force partici-pation can only be one piece of the puzzle of growth. To understand fully the effect of the increase in labor force participation on growth would require not only taking into account the productivity of labor, but also looking at its allocation across industries and firms from a more disaggregated perspective.

Development accounting[6] shows that LAC's physical and human capital gaps relative to the United States are large, but closing them will not fully equalize incomes. To put into context the contribution of factor accumulation to the recent growth episode in LAC, it is instructive to see how much of the region's income gap relative to the United States is because of a capital or efficiency gap. The result of such a hypothetical exercise[7] is displayed in figure 2.7. The lower (shaded) areas of the bars depict the actual observed income per worker in LAC countries relative to the United States (in 2005). The overall bars in figure 2.7 show a counterfactual income level assuming that the economies in LAC would use their human and physical capital as efficiently as the United States does. The remaining difference, almost 60 percent on average, is because of differences in human and physical capital accumulation. This is a surprisingly large magnitude. But it is not sufficient to explain fully the differences in incomes. Assuming that countries in LAC used the capital structure as efficiently as in the United States would certainly increase income per worker, especially for countries such as Bolivia, Ecuador, Guyana, Haiti, Honduras, and Nicaragua. On average, LAC's income per worker would roughly double if the region used its production factors as efficiently as the United States does. LAC thus suffers from an efficiency gap almost as much as it suffers from a capital gap.

FIGURE 2.7: **Decomposition of the Income Gap**

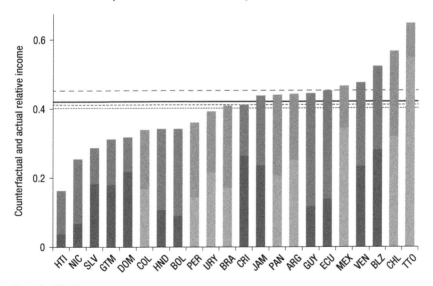

Source: Caselli 2016.
Note: ARG = Argentina; BLZ = Belize; BOL = Bolivia; BRA = Brazil; CHL = Chile; COL = Colombia; CRI = Costa Rica; DOM = Dominican Republic; ECU = Ecuador; GTM = Guatemala; GUY = Guyana; HND = Honduras; HTI = Haiti; JAM = Jamaica; MEX = Mexico; NIC = Nicaragua; PAN = Panama; PER = Peru; SLV = El Salvador; TTO = Trinidad and Tobago; URY = Uruguay; VEN = República Bolivariana de Venezuela.

Notes

1. In figure 2.1, economies with population less than one million (as of 2000) are shown in gray.
2. Even if the determinants of growth varied in a systematic, global fashion, this would imply that all countries would lie on a straight line. For example, assuming a simple unconditional convergence model, this would predict that all countries lie on a straight line that is somewhat steeper than the 45-degree line.
3. However, the sample size for the larger economies is small (N = 18).
4. This is the R-squared from a simple regression of post-2000 growth on a constant and growth in the previous period.
5. Other studies with a more narrow focus include Cole et al. (2005); Daude and Fernandez-Arias (2010); and Ferreira, Pessoa, and Veloso (2012).
6. See Caselli (2008, 1, online version): "Level accounting (more recently known as development accounting) consists of a set of calculations whose purpose is to find the relative contributions of differences in inputs and differences in the efficiency with which inputs are used to cross-country differences in GDP. It is therefore the cross-country analogue of growth accounting."
7. See Caselli (2016) for details.

References

Azevedo, Joao Pedro, Gabriela Inchauste, Sergio Olivieri, Jaime Saavedra, and Hernan Winkler. 2013. "Is Labor Income Responsible for Poverty Reduction? A Decomposition Approach." Policy Research Working Paper 6414, World Bank Group, Washington, DC.

Böwe, Uwe, and Catherine Guillemineau. 2006. "Determinants of Business Cycle Synchronisation across Euro Area Countries." ECB Working Paper No. 587. European Central Bank, Frankfurt, Germany.

Caselli, Francesco. 2008. "Level Accounting." In *The New Palgrave Dictionary of Economics*, second edition, edited by S. N. Durlauf and L. E. Blume. Basingstoke, UK: Palgrave MacMillan.

———. 2016. "The Latin American Efficiency Gap." In *Understanding Latin America and the Caribbean's Income Gap*, edited by J. Araujo, M. Clavijo, E. Vostroknutova, and K. Wacker. Washington, DC: World Bank.

Cole, H. L., L. E. Ohanian, A. Riascos, and J. A. Schmitz, Jr. 2005. "Latin America in the Rearview Mirror." *Journal of Monetary Economics* 52 (1): 69–107.

Daude, C., and E. Fernandez-Arias. 2010. "On the Role of Productivity and Factor Accumulation in Economic Development and the Caribbean." IDB Working Paper Series 155, Inter-American Development Bank, Washington, DC.

Dollar, David, Tatjana Kleineberg, and Aart Kraay. 2016. "Growth Still Is Good for the Poor." *European Economic Review* 81 (1): 68–85.

Ferreira, P. C., S. A. Pessoa, and F. Veloso. 2012. "On the Evolution of Total Factor Productivity in Latin America." *Economic Inquiry* 51 (1): 16–30.

Loayza, Norman, Pablo Fajnzylber, and César Calderón. 2005. *Economic Growth in Latin America and the Caribbean: Stylized Facts, Explanations, and Forecasts.* Washington, DC: World Bank Group.

Sosa, Sebastián. 2010. "The Influence of 'Big Brothers': How Important Are Regional Factors for Uruguay?" IMF Working Paper 10-60, International Monetary Fund, Washington, DC.

3
Modeling Economic Growth and Baseline Results

Drivers of Economic Growth

Previous studies have identified the potential drivers of economic growth. How countries increase their growth rate and thus income per capita has occupied several generations of economists. As Lucas (1988) comments: "Once you start to think about growth, it is hard to think about anything else."[1] This report builds on this vast literature in the empirical model, by taking into account variables that have been suggested as key for economic growth by previous theoretical and empirical studies.[2]

Structural factors are expected to influence long-run aggregate supply. In basic neoclassical long-run models, output per capita is determined by the long-run aggregate supply curve based on an aggregate production function, including capital accumulation and technology (including human capital). In the empirical model, structural policy variables reflecting, for example, human capital, financial development, infrastructure, or trade openness proxy for these effects. Furthermore, the analysis considers institutional quality and government consumption, which might affect capital formation and allocative efficiency.

But cyclical factors and stabilization policies have potential effects on growth as well. Over shorter time horizons, demand factors also have to be taken into account. For example, expansive monetary policy can boost output in the short run. However, its feedback loop through higher inflationary pressure will induce cyclical distortions in the economy that might adversely affect the allocation of factors. Ensuring a stable macroeconomic environment will thus support the most efficient allocation of resources (similar to institutional stability and a level regulatory playing field).[3] In the empirical model, stabilization policies, such as the inflation rate, a proxy for exchange rate misalignment, and banking crisis reflect this channel.

Especially for emerging and developing economies, external conditions might matter. Virtually all developing countries are commodity exporters, so higher prices for their exports (as observed over the past decade) will impact their income via export revenues. Although such commodity price booms might only have a temporary impact, they can also influence long-term aggregate supply if spent wisely, for example in building institutions.[4] Similarly, abundant international liquidity eases access to finance and hence supports capital accumulation in capital-scarce countries. In the empirical model, terms-of-trade growth, growth in (country-specific) commodity prices, and time dummies (capturing global effects such as liquidity) capture these external conditions.

The goal of this report is to identify and quantify these different effects for growth in Latin America and the Caribbean (LAC). Given the strong growth performance in most countries in LAC over the past decade amid a period of booming commodity prices, the aim is to quantify how much of the observed growth can be explained by external factors as opposed to different domestic innovations and improvements. This analysis requires an empirical estimation strategy that can distinguish mere correlation from economic causation.

In line with the focus of the study, the analysis looks at broad aggregate potential drivers of growth to investigate to what extent they can explain the patterns of growth observed over the past decade, and inform policy going forward. This approach puts the study closer to what Cohen and Easterly (2009) term the "Thinking Big" approach. This is not to say that the macro-level approach is the only valid or even best one to understand and promote growth. Given the rich diversity among countries in LAC and recent progress in microeconometrics, the study can add a particular piece of evidence. However, the possible hypothesis that growth in the overall region was mostly driven by broad external factors suggests that it would be useful to take an aggregate macro view.

The study relies on current state-of-the-art techniques to avoid the most common pitfalls in growth regressions. Nevertheless, the findings should be seen as a starting point to investigate in more detail which policies might work, how, in which countries, and for what reasons. For motivating such more tailored investigations, even the observation of mere correlations in macro data can be (and often has been) useful. In that sense, the study does not take a strong stance on whether policy should be based on macro or micro evidence. The key point is that policy should be evidence-based, and accordingly this study aims to contribute to this effort.[5]

Model of the Drivers of Economic Growth

An organizing framework for understanding the drivers of growth needs to align theory and an empirical model. Although economic theory might lead to clear implications about the drivers of growth, it is often not fully feasible to assess them empirically in view of the available data or empirical methods. For example, some variables, such as human capital or financial development, might not be perfectly measurable. Furthermore, some variables (such as demographics) might influence growth in the very long run, whereas other variables (such as exchange rate misalignment or demand components more generally) have a shorter-run effect, leading to a trade-off in the most appropriate empirical model. These considerations highlight the complex relationship between economic theory and empirical assessment.[6]

The focus of this study is the drivers of growth over a policy-relevant horizon. To smooth out most of the cyclical short-run effects, which are not sustainable, the model is estimated with five-year averages of non-overlapping panel data for a sample of 126 countries for 1970–2010. Mainly building on the econometric approach of Loayza, Fajnzylber, and Calderón (2005), the model is set up as a dynamic model (with a lagged dependent variable) for income per capita, which accommodates longer-run effects beyond the five-year interval.[7] Furthermore, this representation allows for efficient estimation of the model in the following form:

$$\ln y_{ct} = \theta \ln y_{ct-1} + \Gamma \ln(X)_{ct} + a_c + b_t + e_{ct} \qquad (3.1)$$

where $\ln y_{ct}$ is the natural log of real purchasing power parity (PPP) gross domestic product (GDP) per capita of country c in period t; X_{ct} is a vector of growth determinants; a_c and b_t are country and year fixed effects, respectively; and e_{ct} is an error term.

Consistent with the goal of gauging the drivers of growth in the past decade, the analysis identifies the parameters over time. Over the past decades, several econometric methods have emerged to estimate growth regressions. (Appendix A provides further details.) A key distinction between these methods is how they identify the relevant parameters. Although some strands in the literature (such as Cohen and Easterly 2009, and Hauk and Wacziarg 2009) favor the use of long-run variations across countries, the current study falls into the camp that uses the variation of variables over time to identify the parameters of interest. Among other advantages, this approach allows for effective estimation of the effects of potential growth drivers that show considerable variation over time but do not vary as much across given countries, such as commodity export prices.

However, the approach does not allow for explicitly assessing the impact of long-run growth drivers that do not vary (much) over time. Factors such as geography, climate, culture, legal origin, or institutions might matter a lot for growth in the long run. But as these factors change little over time, their explicit identification is beyond the scope of this study, which takes a closer look at the drivers of growth in LAC over the past decade. The method of using country fixed effects implicitly controls for all time-invariant cross-country heterogeneities, hence alleviating the potential problem of omitted country variables. But it does not explicitly identify their quantitative parameters.

System–general method of moments (system-GMM) estimation of the levels equation provides efficient and unbiased parameter estimates. Although the model in equation 3.1 explains income per capita, as opposed to growth, the representation in levels allows for more efficient estimation than alternative instrumental variable estimators.[8] By using internal instruments, the system-GMM estimator avoids endogeneity bias of the lagged dependent and explanatory variables.[9] Furthermore, the representation is well-founded in neoclassical growth theory (for details, see Brueckner 2014) and able to evaluate the effects on growth rates. Therefore, equation 3.1 can also be expressed as:

$$\ln y_{ct} - \ln y_{ct-1} = \varphi \ln y_{ct-1} + \Gamma \ln(X)_{ct} + a_c + b_t + e_{ct} \qquad (3.2)$$

where $\varphi = \theta - 1$ $\ln y_{ct} - \ln y_{ct-1}$ is the change in the natural log of real PPP GDP per capita in country c between period t and period $t-1$, that is, the growth rate of per capita GDP.

Consistent with the standard neoclassical growth model, a change in variable X has a permanent effect on income level, but only a transitory effect on income growth. In the model, a permanent perturbation in the level of X has a temporary (short-run) effect on growth in GDP per capita. There is a permanent (long-run) effect on the level of GDP per capita, but not on the GDP per capita growth rate. This is consistent with most neoclassical growth models, as only an improvement in the *growth rate* of fundamental drivers of growth (such as technological progress) will have a permanent effect on the economic growth rate. Similarly, a permanent increase in commodity price *levels* will have an effect on commodity exporters' *income levels*, but no effect on growth rates beyond the transition period from the old to the new income level. In this representation, it would be expected that $\varphi < 0$, that is, countries that are temporarily below their long-run potential output (reflected in the fixed effect a_c) at the beginning of a five-year interval are expected to grow faster in the period ahead, given their steady-state explanatory variables X. This can be described as "cyclical reversion" or "convergence to a country's own steady state," and should not be confused with income convergence across countries. Furthermore, when assessing the contributions of innovations in X to growth (as in this report), the analysis first-differences equation 3.1, which makes the lagged dependent variable become a growth-persistent parameter.[10]

Data from different sources proxy for the growth drivers. Table 3.1 provides a list and summary statistics of the main variables of the model. Table 3.2 displays their bivariate correlations.[11] These pairwise correlations depict how strongly correlated individual variables are with each other.

TABLE 3.1: **Univariate Descriptive Statistics, 1970–2010**
(five-year non-overlapping panel)

Variable	Mean	SD	Min	Max	Observations
Growth rate of GDP per capita	0.096	0.168	−1.086	1.659	1494
Lagged GDP per capita	8.267	12.740	5.272	11.346	1494
Schooling	3.765	0.904	−1.434	5.103	1232
Credit/GDP	3.261	0.939	−0.003	5.544	1259
Trade openness	4.077	0.706	0.552	6.036	1494
Telephone lines	1.291	1.944	−3.975	4.491	1389

(continued on next page)

Variable	Mean	SD	Min	Max	Observations
Government size	2.304	0.625	−0.205	4.165	1494
Polity2	0.976	7.256	−10.000	10.000	1174
CPI inflation	2.214	1.069	−1.753	8.859	1293
Real exchange rate	4.119	0.608	2.137	18.640	1494
Banking crisis	0.056	0.184	0.000	1.000	1494
Terms of trade growth	−0.005	0.211	−1.291	0.652	684
ComPI growth	0.003	0.009	−0.023	0.092	1219

Note: ComPI = international commodity export price index; CPI = consumer price index; GDP = gross domestic product; SD = standard deviation.

Baseline Model

The variables in the baseline model exhibit the expected effects on economic growth, with stabilization policies being on the borderline of statistical significance. As expected, there is strong persistence in income levels, transforming into growth reversals (convergence to the steady state) if the results are interpreted in terms of equation 3.2. As discussed in more detail in chapter 5, structural policies mostly have the expected and statistically significant effects on income and transitory growth rates. Stabilization policies show the expected signs as well, but are not statistically significant in this conditional model, although the standard errors are of reasonable size compared with the estimated parameters. Finally, external conditions, as proxied by the terms of trade and commodity price index, have the expected and highly significant effects on income and transitory growth (see chapter 4 for a discussion).

Several key conclusions emerge from analysis of the factors that affected the region's growth performance in the 2000s. The findings suggest that LAC does not differ greatly from other regions in the world in its main determinants of growth. Furthermore, even after controlling for commodity price dynamics, structural policies continued to play a significant and relevant role in LAC's growth in the 2000s (as they did in the 1990s), suggesting that there was more to the region's recent growth than the commodity boom. However, stabilization policies are found to have played a smaller role in explaining growth more recently than was found in Loayza, Fajnzylber, and Calderón (2005). The difference might be because in the 2000s many countries in LAC had already achieved stable macroeconomic conditions for some time, and therefore other factors became key drivers of growth. The economic magnitudes of the different drivers of growth are depicted in figure 3.1. However, looking at individual

TABLE 3.2: **Bivariate Correlations, 1970–2010**
(five-year non-overlapping panel, 126 countries, 464 observations)

Variable	Growth rate of GDP per capita	Lagged GDP per capita	Schooling	Credit/ GDP	Trade openness	Telephone lines	Polity2	Government size	CPI inflation	Real exchange rate	Banking crisis	Terms of trade growth	ComPI growth
Growth rate of GDP per capita	1.00												
Lagged GDP per capita	0.14	1.00											
Schooling	0.29	0.78	1.00										
Credit/GDP	0.19	0.67	0.62	1.00									
Trade openness	0.25	0.26	0.32	0.22	1.00								
Telephone lines	0.31	0.89	0.87	0.71	0.30	1.00							
Polity2	0.07	0.40	0.44	0.30	0.06	0.47	1.00						
Government size	-0.06	-0.33	-0.39	-0.24	0.03	-0.34	-0.16	1.00					
CPI inflation	-0.20	-0.20	-0.14	-0.40	-0.29	-0.23	-0.08	-0.00	1.00				
Real exchange rate	-0.12	0.36	0.14	0.28	0.01	0.20	0.02	-0.20	-0.08	1.00			
Banking crisis	-0.12	0.15	0.12	0.12	-0.15	0.09	0.12	-0.12	0.20	0.13	1.00		
Terms of trade growth	0.31	0.11	0.14	-0.00	0.17	0.13	0.02	0.01	-0.09	0.03	-0.12	1.00	
ComPI growth	0.17	0.27	0.19	-0.02	0.27	0.18	-0.15	-0.04	0.02	0.07	-0.14	0.40	1.00

Note: ComPI = international commodity export price index; CPI = consumer price index; GDP = gross domestic product.

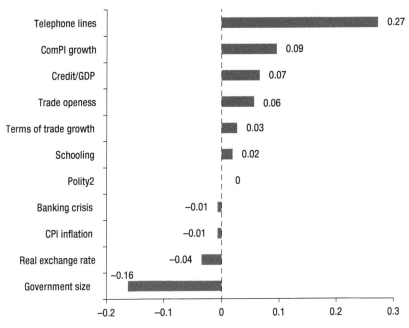

FIGURE 3.1: **Effects of Policies on Economic Growth in LAC**
(estimated coefficients multiplied by standard deviations)

Source: Brueckner 2014.
Note: Values are the growth effect in percent/100, occurring from an average change in the explanatory variable by one standard deviation. ComPI = international commodity export price index; CPI = consumer price index; GDP = gross domestic product.

country-level results, there is a great deal of heterogeneity in the contributions of different drivers of growth within the region. This heterogeneity will be discussed in more detail in subsequent chapters.

Diagnostic Checks

The model works well on aggregated data, comparing the actual and predicted growth rates. In figure 3.1, predicted GDP per capita growth is generated with the estimated coefficients from column 1 in table 3.3 and the observed changes in each of the right-hand-side variables for each time period with the available data (see box 3.1). Figure 3.2 reports average predictions for (i) all countries in the sample, (ii) all countries excluding LAC, and (iii) LAC countries only. Qualitatively, the predictions have the right signs for all time periods and regions. Quantitatively, the predictions are also fairly close to the actual values. For example, the actual average change in log GDP per capita for all countries in the sample over a five-year horizon between 2006–10 and 2001–05 is 0.16 log point, while the predicted change is 0.17 log point; over a 10-year horizon between 2006–10 and 1996–2000, the actual average change is 0.21 log point, while the predicted change is 0.22 log point (figure 3.3).

TABLE 3.3: **Baseline Regression Results**
(conditional effects, five-year unbalanced panel)

Variable	(1)	(2)
	SYS-GMM	LS
ln(GDP p.c.), t-1	0.78***	0.75***
	(0.06)	(0.03)
Structural policies and institutions		
ln(secondary school enrollment rate), t	0.02	−0.03
	(0.05)	(0.03)
ln(private domestic credit/GDP), t	0.07***	0.02
	(0.03)	(0.02)
ln(structure adjusted trade volume/GDP), t	0.08*	0.10***
	(0.05)	(0.03)
ln(government consumption/GDP), t	−0.26***	−0.13***
	(0.04)	(0.03)
ln(telephone lines p.c.), t	0.14***	0.08***
	(0.03)	(0.02)
Polity2 score, t	−0.00	−0.01
	(0.03)	(0.02)
Stabilization policies		
Inflation rate, t	−0.01	−0.01*
	(0.01)	(0.01)
ln(real exchange rate), t	−0.06	−0.02
	(0.04)	(0.03)
Banking crisis, t	−0.04	−0.05*
	(0.03)	(0.03)
External conditions		
ComPI growth, t	10.48***	6.96***
	(2.69)	(2.59)
Terms of trade growth, t	0.12***	0.11***
	(0.03)	(0.03)
AR (1) test, p-value	0.02	—

(continued on next page)

TABLE 3.3: **Baseline Regression Results** *(continued)*

Variable	(1)	(2)
	SYS-GMM	LS
AR (2) test, p-value	0.10	–
Sargan test $\chi^2(10)$, p-value	0.13	–
Country FE	Yes	Yes
Year FE	Yes	Yes
Observations	464	464
Countries	126	126

Note: The dependent variable is real GDP per capita, ln(GDP p.c.). The method of estimation is system-GMM (SYS-GMM) in column 1 and least squares (LS) in column 2. The system-GMM estimation is based on 10 endogenous variables and 20 instruments. AR = auto-regressive; ComPI = international commodity export price index; FE = fixed effects; GDP = gross domestic product; p.c. = per capita.
*Significantly different from zero at the 10 percent significance level, ** 5 percent significance level, *** 1 percent significance level.

BOX 3.1: **Interpreting the Regression Parameters**

The regression model underlying table 3.3 shows the effects of a change in the explanatory variables on the level of income, conditional on other factors. The model setup has several implications for interpreting the parameters:

- The effects do not take into account indirect effects through other channels included in the model. For example, financial development could be a channel through which schooling affects gross domestic product (GDP) per capita growth (say, because education is needed for the functioning of courts, and well-functioning courts are necessary for the enforcement of financial contracts). Since schooling and financial development are included in the model, the estimated coefficient on schooling captures the (residual) effect that schooling has on GDP per capita growth beyond its effect via financial development. However, unconditional effects are also reported for the explanatory variables, and they are used, for example, to derive the benchmarks in the second part of chapter 7.

- The model is set up in levels of income, with a lagged dependent variable. Appendix A demonstrates that the effect on growth (instead of the effect on income) can be derived from this setup.

- A change in the level of an explanatory variable has a permanent effect on income, but a temporary effect on growth.

(continued on next page)

BOX 3.1: Interpreting the Regression Parameters *(continued)*

- The lagged dependent variable captures the persistence of shocks over a five-year period. The estimated coefficient on lagged (log) GDP per capita is 0.78. The estimated coefficient is derived from a five-year non-overlapping panel. The coefficient thus reflects the persistence of shocks to GDP per capita over a five-year horizon. Measured over a one-year horizon, the implied persistence parameter is 0.95 and the implied annual steady-state convergence rate is around 5 percent.

FIGURE 3.2: Economic Growth Regressions
(actual versus predicted growth)

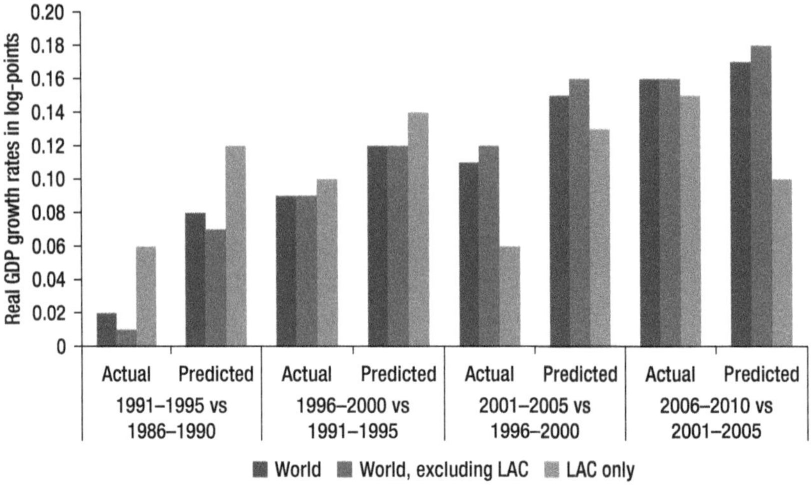

Source: Brueckner 2014.

Standard tests indicate that the baseline model is well-specified. Column 1 in table 3.3 presents the baseline system-GMM estimates.[12] The results do not conflict with theoretical expectations of the drivers of growth, and are consistent with the notion of convergence. However, because of the presence of country fixed effects, this convergence is to countries' own steady states.[13] Standard statistical tests, such as the Sargan test for joint validity of the instrument set or the Arellano-Bond test for serial correlation, indicate that the model is well-specified (see appendix A for details).

FIGURE 3.3: **Actual and Predicted Change in log GDP per Capita, 2006–10 and 1996–2000**
(log points)

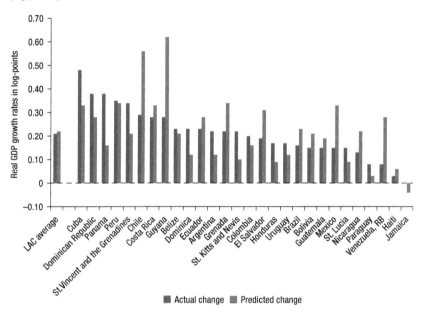

Source: Brueckner 2014.

The following chapters use this model to discuss LAC's key drivers of growth and policy challenges. Figure 3.1 uses overall standard deviations to calculate growth effects, which does not necessarily reveal what has driven growth in LAC specifically. Chapter 4 thus takes a more detailed look at the role of external factors in LAC's growth performance. Chapter 5 moves toward the relevance of domestic factors, especially stabilization and structural policies. In both cases, the baseline model is used to assess the specific contributions of each variable to the growth rate of each country in LAC. Similarly, chapter 6 uses the model to predict what would happen to growth in LAC if recent trends were extended into the future. Given the high reliance on this model, appendix A also demonstrates the robustness of the model to several alternative specifications. Furthermore, chapter 7 identifies those variables where individual countries in LAC lag the most behind their peers, thus highlighting policy areas where constraints are most binding and growth-promoting progress could be achieved relatively easily. Chapter 8 then puts more detailed focus on policy priorities. Chapter 9 concludes.

Notes

1. The full quotation is as follows: "The consequences for human welfare involved in questions like these [about income and growth] are simply staggering: Once one starts to think about them, it is hard to think about anything else" (Lucas 1988, 5).

2. For a textbook treatment and overview, see Romer (2011). Largely following the related study of Loayza, Fajnzylber, and Calderón (2005) in the empirical model setup and variable choice mitigates the potential problem of data mining in the growth regressions. As Cohen and Easterly (2009, 3) note, having a long list of potential explanatory variables to play with makes it easy enough to obtain significant results and arrive at pre-desired conclusions.

3. Chapter 6 discusses and assesses the relation between short-run fluctuations, long-run effects, and growth in more detail.

4. See, for example, Arezki and Brueckner (2012) and World Bank (2014).

5. On this discussion, see especially the volume by Cohen and Easterly (2009) and the discussion by Klenow therein. Araujo et al. (2016) takes a more granular approach toward the drivers of growth and convergence in LAC, looking, for example, at firm-level data and technology adoption. Although the chosen methodology is appropriate for the objectives of this study, the empirical method is by no means an endorsement of any particular approach to development. The benchmarking exercise shows that the path to development differs in each case, and so will the most effective policies to achieve "big chunks" (for example, providing communications infrastructure will work better with liberalization, public-private partnerships in some countries, or public investment in others). Given that the focus is regional, rather than country-specific, and that LAC is a very heterogeneous region, it was not the intention of the study to arrive at specific policy recommendations.

6. A discussion of this relationship is provided in Spanos (1993).

7. A contemporaneous effect of any variable on current income will also impact future income via the lagged dependent variable. While the contemporaneous (short-run) effect is given directly by Γ, the overall (long-run) effect is derived as $\Gamma/(1-\theta)$.

8. An example is the Arellano-Bond first-difference GMM estimator.

9. For example, some of the explanatory variables, X_{ct}, may themselves be a function of the dependent variable, and dynamic panel estimation in the presence of country fixed effects generally yields biased estimates (Nickell 1981; Wooldridge 2002). Therefore, the endogenous variables (in levels) are instrumented with lags of their first differences. The instrument set is limited to one lag, to ensure that the number of instruments does not grow too large in the system-GMM estimation, and furthermore to avoid overfitting the model by using the "collapse" suboption in the STATA *xtabond2* command. The one-step (as opposed to the two-step) estimator is used to avoid severely downward biased standard errors associated with the two-step estimator (Blundell and Bond 1998). See Brueckner (2014) for further details and discussion.

10. The intuition for this fact is as follows: in the first-difference equation $\Delta \ln y_{ct} = \theta(\Delta \ln y_{ct-1}) + \Gamma \Delta \ln(X)_{ct} + \Delta b_t + \Delta e_{ct}$, only contemporary changes in X have an effect on the growth rate. Previous interventions, however, are expected to be reflected in the lagged growth rate, $\Delta \ln y_{ct-1}$, and contribute via this channel to current growth.

11. Appendix table B.1 provides a detailed description of the variables and their sources. Appendix table B.2 provides a list of countries and the number of observations for each variable.

12. These estimates are based on an unbalanced panel covering 126 countries during 1970–2010. Appendix table B.9 shows that the instruments in the system-GMM estimation are relevant: lagged changes have a highly significant effect on levels (panel A), and lagged levels have a highly

significant effect on changes (panel B). The p-value from the Sargan test is greater than 0.1. Hence, we cannot reject the hypothesis of a correctly specified model.

13. In this model, convergence in income per capita is to each country's own steady state, because country fixed effects are used. But because of the inclusion of time fixed effects, which account for U.S. growth and common external shocks, all the results presented are identical to the model with convergence to a common steady state (see appendix table B.8).

References

Araujo, J. T., E. Vostroknutova, K. Wacker, and M. Clavijo, eds. 2016. *Understanding the Income and Efficiency Gap in Latin America and the Caribbean*. Directions in Development Series. Washington, DC: World Bank.

Arellano, M., and S. R. Bond. 1991. "Some Tests of Specification for Panel Data: Monte Carlo Evidence and an Application to Employment Equations." *Review of Economic Studies* 58 (2): 277–97.

Arezki, R., and M. Brueckner. 2012. "Commodity Windfalls, Democracy, and External Debt." *Economic Journal* 122: 848–66.

Blundell, R., and S. Bond. 1998. "Initial Conditions and Moment Restrictions in Dynamic Panel Data Models." *Journal of Econometrics* 87: 115–43.

Brueckner, M. 2014. Background paper for this report. Mimeo. World Bank Group, Washington, DC.

Cohen, Jessica, and William Easterly, eds. 2009. *What Works in Development? Thinking Big and Thinking Small*. Washington, DC: Brookings Institution Press.

Hauk, W., and R. Wacziarg. 2009. "A Monte Carlo Study of Growth Regressions." *Journal of Economic Growth* 14: 103–47.

Loayza, Norman, Pablo Fajnzylber, and César Calderón. 2005. *Economic Growth in Latin America and the Caribbean: Stylized Facts, Explanations, and Forecasts*. Washington, DC: World Bank Group.

Lucas, Jr., Robert. 1988. "On the Mechanics of Economic Development." *Journal of Monetary Economics* 22: 3–42.

Nickell, S. 1981. "Biases in Dynamic Models with Fixed Effects." *Econometrica* 49: 1417–26.

Romer, David. 2011. *Advanced Macroeconomics*. 4th edition. New York: McGraw-Hill.

Spanos, Aris. 1993. *Statistical Foundations of Economic Modelling*. Cambridge: Cambridge University Press.

Wooldridge, J. 2002. *Econometric Analysis of Cross Section and Panel Data*. Cambridge, MA: MIT Press.

World Bank. 2014. *Diversified Development: Making the Most of Natural Resources in Eurasia*. Washington, DC: World Bank.

4

Role of External Factors

How Did External Factors Affect Growth in LAC?

The growth pickup in Latin America and the Caribbean (LAC) coincided with favorable external conditions. The relatively high growth rates in LAC in the past decade took place against a combination of high commodity prices, low world interest rates, and abundant international liquidity. These were unprecedented tailwinds for developing countries, which are mostly commodity exporters and dependent on external financing. Commodity export prices (energy and non-energy) increased dramatically after the early 2000s. For most countries in LAC, this increase implied a considerable improvement in terms of trade. In addition, financial conditions in the United States were relatively loose, making financing costs and market access quite favorable for countries in LAC. After the dot-com bubble and again after the global financial crisis, unconventional and supportive monetary policy in high-income economies led to relatively favorable financing conditions for emerging economies. These external conditions were correlated with growth in LAC, as shown in figure 4.1. With annual data for 2000–12, the correlation coefficients of average LAC growth with U.S. financial conditions and non-energy commodity price changes were relatively high (0.56 and 0.82, statistically significant at the 5 and 1 percent levels, respectively); however, correlation does not necessarily imply a causal relationship.

Compared with other regions, commodity price effects were not significantly different for LAC. There is no parameter heterogeneity present between LAC and other countries in the impact of external factors on growth. In addition, figure 4.2 depicts that the external tailwinds were not significantly different for the LAC region, as shown by the overlapping 95 percent confidence bands. Commodity price booms require an adequate institutional setup to have a positive impact on long-term growth, highlighting the role that earlier improvements in stabilization policies might have played in LAC (box 4.1).

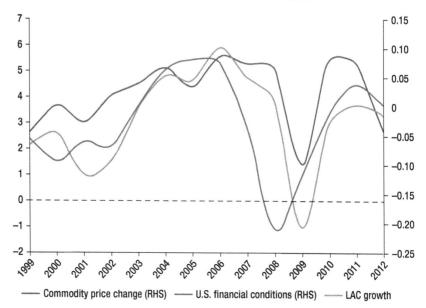

Source: World Bank Group staff calculations; Haver Analytics; Wacker, Lodge, and Nicoletti 2014.
Note: The left-hand-side y-axis is the U.S. Financial Conditions Index; it is an absolute value (divided by 10 to rescale) showing how loose or tight U.S. financial conditions are (relative to 0). The right-hand-side axis is the commodity price change, which is the annual percentage change (so 0.1 would be a year-on-year 10 percent increase). LAC growth is an (unweighted) average of 32 countries in the region. LAC = Latin America and the Caribbean; RHS = right-hand side.

The regression model confirms that external conditions had a positive impact on growth in LAC. Variations in countries' terms of trade and international commodity export prices had a positive and statistically significant impact on growth. Because the terms of trade and international commodity export price index are country-specific variables, the estimated coefficients on these variables capture the country-specific effects of external conditions. Figure 4.2 shows that the economic growth of countries was also considerably affected by common factors.[1] The figure shows that there were significant tailwinds in the past decade.

The contribution of external factors was as important as that of structural policies for growth in LAC, on average. Figure 4.3 disaggregates the growth rates the model estimates for all countries in LAC over the past decade into individual contributions by main variable categories. For the LAC average, the figure shows that the contribution of external factors was the same as that of structural policies, at 0.5 percentage points per year; stabilization policies had no impact; and growth persistence contributed 1.2 percentage points per year. These findings suggest that over the past decade external conditions contributed substantially to growth in LAC. This was especially true for resource-rich countries, such as Chile, Guyana, and República Bolivariana de

(estimated coefficients and confidence intervals)

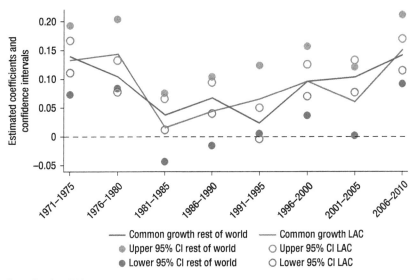

Source: Brueckner 2014.
Note: CI = confidence interval; LAC = Latin America and the Caribbean.

BOX 4.1: **How Can a Commodity Boom Drive a Virtuous Cycle of Growth?**

Commodity price booms can have a positive impact on growth via various channels. As schematically depicted in figure B4.1.1, a commodity price boom directly raises domestic income via terms-of-trade effects. Since commodity exporters are mostly capital-scarce, this might foster investment by lowering the relative costs of inputs, such as machines, thereby overcoming existing supply bottlenecks and generating solid ground for future growth. Similarly, as public enterprises usually play a key role in the commodity sector, a commodity price boom helps improve public finances, which in turn can be invested in upgrading public infrastructure. Finally, when exchange rate pass-through is high, higher output does not necessarily come at the cost of higher inflation, because commodity booms tend to appreciate the exchange rate, which in turn might help anchor future inflation expectations.

But the actual growth effects of the commodity boom are controversial, as the boom also poses several macroeconomic challenges. For example, the associated real exchange rate appreciation reduces the international price competitiveness of manufactured

(continued on next page)

goods, potentially eroding a country's productive base (Dutch disease). Furthermore, high public commodity revenues might have a detrimental effect on institutional quality and the efficiency of public spending. It is thus not straightforward that countries can take advantage of a commodity price boom, and this capacity seems to depend critically on the institutional framework in place. For example, structural fiscal rules, as in Chile or Colombia, might prevent the government from overspending during boom periods. This consideration highlights the extent to which the current growth performance in LAC is really driven by commodity prices or by improved macroeconomic policies.

A commodity boom can also trigger a vicious cycle of stagnation, if the typical manifestations of a "resource curse" are observed: government overspending and overborrowing, rent-seeking behavior, and decline of nonbooming tradable sectors.

FIGURE B4.1.1: **Schematic of the Effects of a Commodity Price Boom**

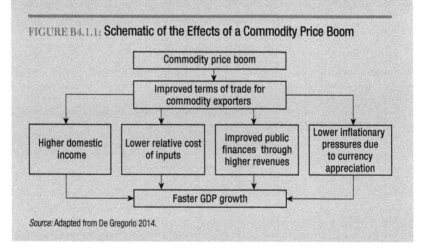

Source: Adapted from De Gregorio 2014.

Venezuela, where growth of average gross domestic product (GDP) per capita during the 2000s was boosted because of positive terms-of-trade developments by over 2 percentage points per year.[2]

Figure 4.3 can be used to assess what would have happened to countries in LAC without the commodity bonanza and other global factors. The parts of the bars in figure 4.3 that represent "external conditions" can be subtracted to assess how growth in LAC would have looked if commodity prices had remained at the level of the late 1990s. On average, the slowdown in growth for the region would have been relatively small, but this should not obscure certain country-specific results. Without the commodity price boom, República Bolivariana de Venezuela, for example, would have completely stagnated, and growth in Chile and Guyana would have been substantially slower (while

FIGURE 4.3: Predicted Growth Effect from Persistence, Policies, and External Conditions

(average growth in 2006–10 relative to average growth in 1996–2000; log points, countries ordered by the contribution of external factors)

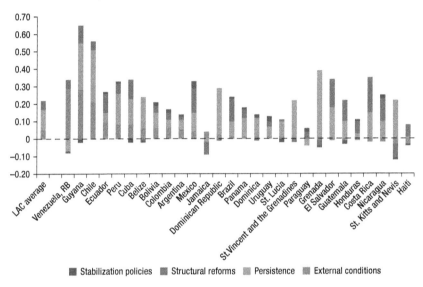

Stabilization policies ■ Structural reforms ■ Persistence ■ External conditions

Source: Brueckner 2014.
Note: To convert into annual changes in percentage points, all values need to be multiplied by 10.

still remaining relatively high). For most other countries, commodity prices played a smaller role; commodity importers would even have benefitted from commodity prices remaining at their late 1990s level. On top of this commodity effect, the analysis could also add the difference in time dummies between periods (such as 1996–2000 and 2006–10) to assess how other global factors contributed to growth in LAC. However, this effect would be small (0.02 log point and statistically insignificant), so most of the external factors should be captured by commodity price and terms-of-trade developments.

Are there potential long-run consequences from the commodity boom?

The commodity boom induced a surge in net commodity exports. A commodity boom can imply adverse effects for growth via a contraction of the manufacturing sector in favor of a considerable increase in net exports of primary commodities. Such an increase in net commodity exports, driven primarily by high commodity prices, was indeed present in LAC over the past decade, as depicted in figure 4.4. Between 2000 and 2012, net commodity exports as a share of GDP in LAC rose from 38.3 percent to 60.9 percent. Similarly, the share of commodities in total exports in LAC increased from 40.0 percent to 54.3 percent over the same period. Increasing reliance on commodity

FIGURE 4.4: **Net Commodity Exports in LAC**
(nominal exports less imports of primary commodities, in percent of
GDP; price index)

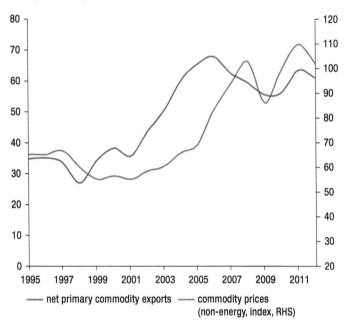

— net primary commodity exports — commodity prices
(non-energy, index, RHS)

Source: World Bank Group staff calculations based on UNCTAD Stats.
Note: LAC = Latin America and the Caribbean; RHS = right-hand side.

exports might give rise to externally-driven vulnerabilities (such as future downward shocks in prices). Furthermore, high commodity revenues may give the government few incentives to establish an efficient tax or institutional system.

Although windfall commodity revenues may impede institutional reforms and negatively affect governance, the negative effects of the commodity boom on institutions in LAC were limited. Several researchers have suggested that natural resource wealth may impede economic growth, as the government may have few incentives to establish an efficient tax or institutional system (Sachs and Warner 1995; Mehlum, Moene, and Torvik 2006). When revenues are high, fewer other income sources are needed, and as citizens pay accordingly fewer taxes, they might demand less representation and accountability. As long as resource revenues are abundant, the government also might not put enough emphasis on efficient spending and governance. And finally, rising commodity prices increase the potential return for political and military incumbents that appropriate those resources, hence potentially inducing political and military conflicts.

How relevant was this potential curse for the LAC region? Looking at the developments in LAC over the commodity boom period, figure 4.5 provides some support for

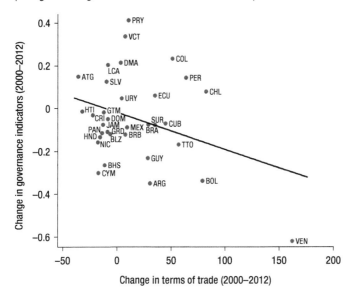

FIGURE 4.5: **Terms of Trade and Governance**
(changes in the governance index and terms of trade)

Source: World Bank Group staff calculations based on World Development Indicators and World Bank Governance Indicators.
Note: ARG = Argentina; ATG = Antigua and Barbuda; BHS = Bahamas; BLZ = Belize; BOL = Bolivia; BRA = Brazil; BRB = Barbados; CHL = Chile; COL = Colombia; CRI = Costa Rica; CUB = Cuba; CYM = Cayman Islands; DMA = Dominica; DOM = Dominican Republic; ECU = Ecuador; GRD = Grenada; GTM = Guatemala; GUY = Guyana; HND = Honduras; HTI = Haiti; JAM = Jamaica; LCA = St. Lucia; MEX = Mexico; NIC = Nicaragua; PAN = Panama; PER = Peru; PRY = Paraguay; SLV = El Salvador; SUR = Suriname; TTO = Trinidad and Tobago; URY = Uruguay; VCT = St. Vincent and the Grenadines; VEN = República Bolivariana de Venezuela.

the negative relationship between commodity export revenues and governance. The figure plots the change in an indicator of governance[3] over 2000–12 against the change in the terms of trade over the same period for LAC economies. The figure shows that, on average, countries that benefitted from a rise in their export prices made less progress in improving governance. The extent of this relationship is especially driven by República Bolivariana de Venezuela, which suffered a dramatic decline in governance indicators amid a period of enormous terms-of-trade increases. Excluding República Bolivariana de Venezuela from the sample, the relationship is essentially zero, although still slightly negative. For the individual governance indicators, the analysis finds that the negative correlation of the terms of trade is strongest with control of corruption and regulatory quality.[4] The dispersion in the relationship depicted in figure 4.5 overall suggests that many factors, other than commodity price developments, impacted institutional performance in LAC over the past decade; moreover, some countries that are not exclusively net commodity exporters performed poorly on institutional reform.

A moderation of commodity prices will pose challenges ahead for many LAC economies. For economies in LAC where external conditions were a main growth factor over the past decade, a moderation of commodity prices in the near future would require tapping into new sources of growth. Institutional progress is a natural candidate for those countries where high commodity revenues have hidden or even fostered shortcomings in governance in the recent past. As the remainder of this report argues in more detail, these countries have no option other than to promote structural policies in the face of receding tailwinds, as structural policies still can have substantial growth effects and will foster economic adjustment beyond commodity exports.

Notes

1. The figure is based on the coefficients and standard errors that were obtained from a regression of GDP per capita growth on time dummies and the interaction of time dummies with an indicator variable for LAC countries.

2. In comparison, the model predicts that average GDP per capita growth (per year) was boosted in these countries because of structural reforms by 0.5, 1.1, and 0.5 percentage points, respectively.

3. This indicator is an average of indicators of the control of corruption, government effectiveness, political stability and absence of violence/terrorism, regulatory quality, and voice and accountability, as constructed by Kaufmann, Kraay, and Mastruzzi (2010).

4. Simple (unconditional) fixed effects regressions for 35 LAC countries are used to assess these relationships. The correlations are negative throughout, but only statistically significant for control of corruption and regulatory quality. In the latter case, however, the results are not robust to excluding República Bolivariana de Venezuela from the sample.

References

Brueckner, M. 2014. Background paper for this report. Mimeo. World Bank Group, Washington, DC.

De Gregorio, J. 2014. *How Latin America Weathered the Global Financial Crisis.* Washington, DC: Peterson Institute for International Economics.

Kaufmann, Daniel, Aart Kraay, and Massimo Mastruzzi. 2010. "The Worldwide Governance Indicators: Methodology and Analytical Issues." Policy Research Working Paper 5430, World Bank, Washington, DC.

Mehlum, Halvor, Karl Moene, and Ragnar Torvik. 2006. "Institutions and the Resource Curse." *Economic Journal* 116 (508): 1–20.

Sachs, Jeffrey D., and Andrew M. Warner. 1995. "Natural Resource Abundance and Economic Growth." NBER Working Paper 5398, National Bureau of Economic Research, Cambridge, MA.

Wacker, K. M., David Lodge, and Giulio Nicoletti. 2014. "Measuring Financial Conditions in Major Non-Euro Area Economies." ECB Working Paper 1743, European Central Bank, Frankfurt, Germany.

5

Role of Domestic Factors

Inflation and Macroeconomic Volatility

Countries were able to use their macroeconomic frameworks to stabilize output and inflation, and support overall stability. Figures 5.1 and 5.2 suggest that the Latin America and the Caribbean (LAC) region has mostly overcome the problems of inflation and macroeconomic volatility that plagued the region in the past. In previous decades, it did not make much sense even to calculate mean inflation in LAC, as the inflation levels in some countries would put them off the chart of any meaningful comparison.[1] Average inflation among countries in LAC was above 100 percent in the 1980s. But, as figure 5.1 illustrates, the days of hyperinflation are largely over. Inflation rates fell in the 1990s compared with the previous decade, although some outliers (most notably Brazil) still existed. During the 2000s, inflation rates fell further. The box plot in figure 5.1 shows that the dispersion of inflation rates has become narrower in the region. The only countries in LAC that have experienced mean inflation rates above 15 percent since 2000 are República Bolivariana de Venezuela and Suriname. The achievements with respect to output stabilization in LAC might also be one of the reasons why growth was especially pro-poor in the past decade (see Crespo-Cuaresma, Klasen, and Wacker 2013).

As a result, growth in LAC has become more resilient to downward shocks. Figure 5.2 suggests that the most progress in overall output stabilization was already achieved in the 1990s and sustained after 2000. Reducing volatility further would be difficult, given that market economies inherently have fluctuations in output. As figure 5.3 further illustrates, contraction periods in LAC became somewhat shorter in the 2000s compared with the 1980s and 1990s.[2] Despite the magnitude of the global financial crisis, the last contraction period in LAC lasted only one year, whereas the recession of the early 1990s and the spillovers from the Asian crisis of 1998 generated longer-lasting declines in gross domestic product (GDP) per capita.[3] Here downward shocks are defined as years with growth rates below the fifth percentile of annual

FIGURE 5.1: Inflation across Latin America and the Caribbean over the Decades

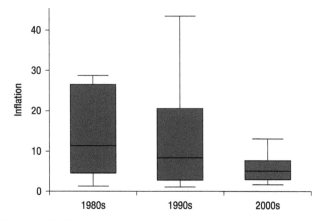

Source: Calculations based on World Development Indicators.

FIGURE 5.2: Growth Volatility across Latin America and the Caribbean over the Decades

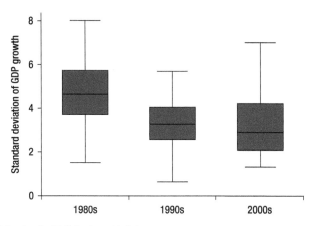

Source: Calculations based on World Development Indicators.

growth for all countries of the world over the period 1980–2012 (which amounts to a threshold of −7 percent per year). In LAC, 26 such shocks happened throughout the 1980s, but only eight occurred in the 1990s and after 2000. These achievements in output stabilization most likely reflect improvements in macroeconomic policies and institutions that most governments in the region promoted during the 1990s.

Peaks and Troughs in the Region's GDP per Capita

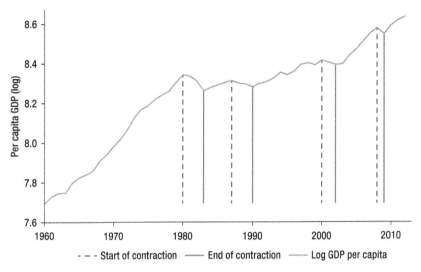

Source: World Bank Group staff calculations based on World Development Indicators.
Note: GDP = gross domestic product.

Impact of Stabilization Policies

The model used in this study suggests that the impact of stabilization policies on growth in LAC was small, relative to the effects of other factors. The coefficients of variables relating to stabilization policies, such as inflation, real exchange rate, and banking crises, are negative although not statistically significant (see table 3.3 in chapter 3). As the coefficients of these variables are obtained from a multivariate regression model, they should be interpreted as conditional effects.[4] These conditional effects may differ from unconditional effects. We will explore unconditional effects. By order of magnitude, the effect of stabilization policies is smaller than that of structural policies (figure 3.1 in chapter 3). A one standard deviation increase in the real exchange rate, inflation, and risk of banking crisis is predicted to decrease five-year GDP per capita growth by around 4, 1, and 1 percentage points, respectively.[5] As figure 5.4 suggests, stabilization policies overall contributed little to LAC's growth performance over the past decade. The average contribution is zero, suggesting that an average country in LAC has approached a plateau on that policy dimension. Only some countries, most notably Mexico and Uruguay, have seen further progress on stabilization that fostered growth over the past decade.

Payoffs to further price and output stabilization are potentially limited in most countries in LAC. Although some LAC countries still have substantial room for improving their stabilization policy, the fruits of the latter have already been reaped by many other economies. This is exemplified by inflation stabilization in figure 5.4, which depicts the relationship between inflation and growth in LAC over the decades. During the 1980s, there was a clear negative relationship between inflation and growth: countries with higher inflation rates grew slower, or even experienced negative growth rates. In the 1990s, the relationship became more complex, being strongly negative for countries with weaker performance but essentially flat for economies that performed well. After 2000, there was no relationship between observed growth and inflation rates in LAC. This does not mean that these countries do not have to care about inflation anymore, especially taking into account that low inflation during this period was influenced by external factors. It is difficult to imagine that LAC would have benefitted as much from the favorable external environment without strong institutional performance. But the relationship suggests that the effects of further reductions in inflation on growth would likely be negligible for many countries in the region (see also Fischer 1993; Khan and Senhadji 2001; Kremer, Bick, and Nautz 2013).

Nevertheless, stabilization policies have significant effects on per capita income growth in an unconditional model that allows their effects to operate via other variables. While previous results from the model were derived from a multivariate (conditional) regression, the study also estimated an unconditional model.[6] Since the variables are included in the model one at a time, the estimated coefficients should be interpreted as

FIGURE 5.4: **Inflation and Growth in LAC over the Decades**

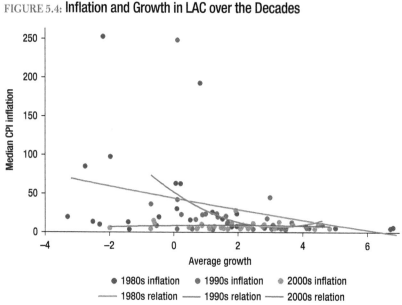

Source: World Bank Group staff calculations based on World Development Indicators.
Note: CPI = consumer price index.

unconditional effects; that is, the effects may operate via other channels that are captured by different variables in the multivariate model. In this setup, inflation, real exchange rate, and banking crises have a significant effect on GDP per capita growth. Since the effects of variables related to stabilization policies are significant in the unconditional model, but not in the multivariate panel estimates, this suggests that stabilization policies also impact growth through other channels. This conclusion is intuitive to the extent that structural and stabilization policies go hand in hand. For example, potential advantages of moderate inflation only materialize in economies where agents trade freely and competitively.

Impact of Structural Policies

Structural policies were a key growth determinant, and had a sizable and significant effect on economic growth in LAC. In contrast to stabilization policies, the estimates from the multivariate regression model support the hypothesis that structural policies are important growth determinants. Variables relating to structural policies, such as financial development, trade openness, and infrastructure, enter with a significant positive coefficient; the size of government enters with a significant negative coefficient. Education and political institutions have a statistically insignificant effect, suggesting that the five-year time frame might be too short to bring about significant variation, that they act mostly through other channels (see balanced panel section), or that the education data have a large measurement error (for example, because educational attainment might not be a strong proxy for actual skills). These results are similar to those obtained from the unbalanced panel, although schooling is mostly significant there, suggesting that it might also have an impact via other channels in the multivariate model.[7]

Figure 3.1 (in chapter 3) facilitates the interpretation of the estimates reported in column 1 in table 3.3 (in chapter 3) by showing the estimated coefficients multiplied by their standard deviations. The product therefore shows the growth effect occurring from an average change in the explanatory variable. The magnitude of the impact that variables relating to structural policies have on economic growth is substantial. For example, a one standard deviation increase in infrastructure, financial development, and trade openness is predicted to increase five-year GDP per capita growth by 27, 7, and 6 percentage points, respectively; a reduction in the size of government of one standard deviation is predicted to increase five-year GDP per capita growth by 16 percentage points.

The relevance of structural policies has been especially large in countries where external conditions contributed little to growth. The predicted contributions of the observed changes in structural policies to growth at the country level (figure 4.3) were most important in Brazil, Costa Rica, El Salvador, Mexico, and Nicaragua. In none of these countries did external conditions contribute much to growth, suggesting that countries that do not benefit as strongly from external tailwinds should have a greater push for structural reform. Structural reforms in some resource-rich countries, such as Chile, Colombia, and Peru during the 2000s, also contributed positively to economic growth, around half a percentage point per year. Interestingly, for Chile, which has long been seen as the paragon of structural reforms in LAC, the estimates suggest that in the 2000s most of the growth was because of persistence, followed by external conditions, while only about 0.5 percent per year of per capita GDP growth was because of structural reforms, and none was because of stabilization policies.[8] By contrast, the Dominican Republic, Grenada, Jamaica, St. Kitts and Nevis, and St. Vincent and the Grenadines are the top five countries where the deterioration in structural reforms contributed negatively to growth.

The relevance of structural policies is robust to different measures of key variables. In line with the empirical growth literature (Mankiw, Romer, and Weil 1992; Loayza, Fajnzylber, and Calderón 2005), the main measure of schooling is the secondary school enrollment rate. Table B.5 in appendix B shows that there is also a positive effect when the analysis uses alternative measures of schooling, such as the primary school enrollment rate or the tertiary enrollment rate. Moreover, there exists a significant positive effect when education is measured by total years of schooling and the model is not conditioned on other variables.[9] Similarly, the main measure of telecommunications infrastructure is the number of telephone lines per capita. In recent decades, mobile phones have become widely used. Hence, mobile phones are another relevant indicator of telecommunications infrastructure. Column 1 in table B.6 in appendix B shows that there is a significant positive effect on GDP per capita growth with this alternative measure of telecommunications infrastructure.

Need for Continued Reform

Continued reform effort is needed to achieve convergence to higher income levels. The estimates in table 3.3 (in chapter 3) should be interpreted as improvements in policies leading to increases in the GDP per capita of the country where these policies are implemented. Given that innovations in the levels of the explanatory variables have a permanent effect on income but a temporary effect on growth, the actual growth effect in the model comes from the innovation (a policy reform), not the level of the explanatory variable. Thus, relatively poor countries that undergo policy improvements will see their income level and associated living standards rise, but growth will only improve as long as this new level is reached. However, observing that poor countries carry out policy reforms does not mean that there will be convergence in incomes across countries. The reason is that the income gap between rich and poor countries not only depends on policies in poor countries, but also on policies in rich countries. If rich countries improve their structural and stabilization policies at a rate faster than poor countries do, then the income gap between rich and poor countries will widen. To make this point clearer, table B.8 in appendix B reports estimates from a model where the dependent variable is countries' GDP per capita relative to the GDP per capita of the

United States. As can be seen, the coefficients on the right-hand-side variables are identical to those of the baseline estimates reported in table 3.3 (in chapter 3).[10]

The estimated impacts of the structural and stabilization policies measured by the model are independent of the common headwinds, such as commodity price dynamics. It is useful to recall that, in the regression model, the common factors are captured by year fixed effects. The coefficients reported in table 3.3 (in chapter 3) on variables related to structural policies and stabilization policies are therefore not driven by common headwinds or tailwinds.

Notes

1. This is also why the analysis looks at the median (and not average) rate of inflation in figure 5.4, as the median is less sensitive than the mean to outliers and skewed distributions.

2. To evaluate the duration of contraction phases, the Harding and Pagan (2002) algorithm was used to determine turning points (peaks or troughs) in yearly GDP per capita (purchasing power parity) with GDP per capita data from the World Development Indicators. The following censoring rules were imposed on the cycle (number of periods in parentheses): window (1), phase (1), and cycle (3).

3. The only country included in the analysis for which there is no evidence of a decline in the duration of economic downturns is Argentina.

4. In table 3.3 (in chapter 3), an F-test on the joint significance of variables in the category of structural reforms (stabilization policies) yields a p-value of 0.00 (0.19) in column 1 and 0.00 (0.08) in column 2, strengthening the interpretation that structural reforms are jointly significant.

5. For comparison with the system–general method of moments (system-GMM) estimates, least squares estimates are reported in column 2 in table 3.3 (in chapter 3). The least squares estimates reveal a qualitatively similar pattern as the system-GMM estimates. Structural policies are significantly correlated with economic growth. And the least squares estimates on variables related to stabilization policies are significant. Quantitatively, the least squares estimates are generally smaller in absolute value than the system-GMM estimates. This finding could in part reflect classical measurement error that leads to an attenuation of least squares estimates but not instrumental variables estimates. Another reason could be endogeneity biases that are corrected for in the system-GMM regression but not in the least squares regression.

6. The unconditional models include the variables of interest one at a time, controlling for lagged GDP as well as country and year fixed effects (see column 1 in table B.4 in appendix B) as well as the international commodity export price index to control for commodity price windfalls (column 2 in table B.4). This estimation strategy has the key advantage that it allows for a much larger sample. Details are available in appendix A.

7. The estimated unconditional effects are also quantitatively sizable. It is useful to recall that the coefficients reported in the tables capture the impact elasticity effects; the cumulative long-run effects can be obtained by dividing these coefficients by $1/1-\theta$, where θ is the coefficient on lagged GDP per capita. For example, for schooling, the estimated coefficient of 0.06 in panel A, column 1 in table B.4 (in appendix B) should be interpreted as a 1 percent increase in the secondary school enrollment rate leading to an increase in GDP per capita over a five-year period of around 0.06 percent; the cumulative long-run effect of a (permanent) increase in the secondary school enrollment rate is larger, over 0.28 percent.

8. However, Chile is one of only a few countries where the model-predicted value is not close to the actual value. Furthermore, this does not imply that structural reform did not promote growth. It simply suggests that less structural reform, as measured by the proxy variables, has taken place in the 2000s, while structural reforms in the 1990s are reflected in the high relevance of growth persistence.

9. This finding agrees with Barro and Lee (2010). Unfortunately, it was not viable to examine at the within-country level the effects of school quality on economic growth. The reason is lack of time-series data. Hanushek and Woessman (2012) argue that Latin American countries have experienced relatively low GDP per capita growth rates over the past half century, despite having relatively high levels of school attainment, because of low educational achievement. The empirical analysis in Hanushek and Woessman (2012) is based entirely on cross-section data.

10. Econometrically, the reason for this is that the baseline model controls for time fixed effects.

References

Barro, R., and J. W. Lee. 2010. "A New Data Set of Educational Attainment in the World, 1950–2010." NBER Working Paper 15902, National Bureau of Economic Research, Cambridge, MA.

Crespo-Cuaresma, Jesús, Stephan Klasen, and Konstantin M. Wacker. 2013. "Why We Don't See Poverty Convergence: The Role of Macroeconomic Volatility." CRC Discussion Paper 153, Courant Research Center, Göttingen, Germany.

Fischer, Stanley. 1993. "The Role of Macroeconomic Factors in Growth," *Journal of Monetary Economics* 32: 485–512.

Hanushek, E., and L. Woessman. 2012. "Schooling, Educational Achievement, and the Latin American Growth Puzzle." *Journal of Development Economics* 99: 497–512.

Harding, Don, and Adrian Pagan. 2002. "Dissecting the Cycle: A Methodological Investigation." *Journal of Monetary Economics* 49: 265–381.

Khan, Moshin S., and Abdelhak S. Senhadji. 2001. "Threshold Effects in the Relationship between Inflation and Growth." *IMF Staff Papers* 48 (1): 1–21.

Kremer, Stephanie, Alexander Bick, Dieter Nautz. 2013. "Inflation and Growth: New Evidence from a Dynamic Panel Threshold Analysis." *Empirical Economics* 44 (2): 861–78.

Loayza, Norman, Pablo Fajnzylber, and César Calderón. 2005. *Economic Growth in Latin America and the Caribbean: Stylized Facts, Explanations, and Forecasts.* Washington, DC: World Bank Group.

Mankiw, G., D. Romer, and D. Weil. 1992. "A Contribution to the Empirics of Economic Growth." *Quarterly Journal of Economics* 107: 407–37.

6
Extensions of the Model

Potential Parameter Heterogeneity

This chapter explores parameter heterogeneity across countries and time. The chapter begins by discussing whether the growth effects of structural and stabilization policies are significantly different in countries in Latin America and the Caribbean (LAC). Econometrically, this question can be examined by adding to the econometric model (in chapter 3) an interaction term between the right-hand-side variables and an indicator variable that is unity for countries in LAC. The coefficient on this interaction term gives the difference in the marginal effect for countries in LAC (relative to the rest). Table B.7 in appendix B shows the relevant results. The main finding is that there is virtually no evidence that the growth effects of structural and stabilization policies are different for countries in LAC compared with other regions of the world. This can be seen from the quantitatively small and statistically insignificant coefficients on the interaction terms between variables relating to policies and the LAC dummy variable.[1,2]

There has been no significant variation in the marginal effects of structural and stabilization policies over time. Another interesting question that can be explored with the panel data model is whether the growth effects of structural and stabilization policies vary over time. Table B.8 in appendix B reports estimates from a model that interacts the variables relating to structural policies and stabilization policies with an indicator variable for the post-1990 period (the midpoint in the sample). Significant coefficients on these interaction terms would suggest that the growth effects of structural and stabilization policies differ for the post-1990 period, that is, are unstable over time. However, the main finding is that the coefficients on the post-1990 interaction terms (reported in column 2) are quantitatively small, especially when measured relative to the coefficients on the linear effects (reported in column 1). Except for lagged gross domestic product (GDP) and infrastructure, the interaction terms are not significantly different from zero. Similar results emerge for the post-2000 period; see table B.8. However, this finding does not imply that the contribution of different policies and country-specific external effects did not vary over time. For example, a variable that might have undergone a substantial change in the past decade but remained fairly stable in the decade before would contribute more to growth in the latter decade, although its effect per unit of change would remain the same.

Potential Complementarities

Complementarities among structural and stabilization features could potentially improve on the in-sample predictions vis-à-vis the baseline model. The idea is to test whether the joint impact of different reforms is greater than the sum of the individual impacts. A "complementarity premium" would result from potential synergies among the distinct drivers of growth Gallego and Loayza (2002). The empirical literature offers some examples of complementarities: foreign direct investment may foster growth in countries with greater human capital Borensztein, De Gregorio, and Lee (1998) or with deeper domestic financial markets Alfaro et al. (2004); the growth benefits from financial openness are reaped by governments with stronger institutions Klein and Olivei (2008); and the benefits from trade growth are greater in countries with greater progress in first- and second-generation reforms Chang, Kaltani, and Loayza (2009). There can be multiple interactions among structural policies and between structural policies and other types of shocks.

Potential policy complementarities are studied through the use of interaction dummies Gallego and Loayza (2002). Specifically, the interaction dummy takes the value 1 if the relevant variable is greater than the world median. Structural variables are interacted with (i) inflation greater than the median; (ii) infrastructure indicator greater than the median; (iii) financial development greater than the median; and (iv) inflation less than the median, plus financial development as well as infrastructure greater than the median. The approach adopted here—defining dummies for variables with values greater than the median and then interacting these with other variables—reduces measurement error and thus attenuates bias. These interactions are instrumented: the product of the instruments used for the linear model and the dummies taking the value 1 if a policy variable is above the median.

However, except for inflation and the real exchange rate, the interaction terms in the expanded model are not found to be significant. Table B.21 in appendix B presents estimates from an interaction model that includes the suggested interaction terms. Column 4 presents the results when the interaction is done with a joint indicator variable (inflation, infrastructure, and financial depth). The main result is that none of the interaction terms is significantly different from zero at the 5 percent level. If the variables in columns 1 to 3 are considered individually to construct the interaction term, then there is also no systematic evidence across the range of structural and stabilization policies of significant heterogeneity. Only for inflation and the real exchange rate is the interaction term significantly different from zero at the 5 percent level. The coefficient on the interaction with (above median) financial depth is positive, suggesting that inflation and appreciation of the real exchange rate are less harmful for growth at higher levels of financial development.

Beyond the Short-Run/Long-Run Dichotomy: Alternative Stabilization Measures

Modern macroeconomics emphasizes the role of short-run fluctuations for long-run growth. Empirical research has stressed the role of volatility in long-run growth.[3] This issue has become especially relevant for the debate about the long-run consequences of the current depression. More generally, the new synthesis in macroeconomics strives to analyze short-run fluctuations and long-run growth within a single consistent framework.[4] This section thus takes a deeper look at the variables to approximate macroeconomic fluctuations. More precisely, the analysis looks at the output gap at the beginning of each five-year period, which is measured as the difference between actual output and output estimated with an HP filter. This gap is expected to have a positive impact on growth because of "cyclical reversion." Furthermore, the analysis looks at GDP volatility, which is expected to have a negative impact on growth and is measured as the standard deviation of the cyclical component obtained from HP filtering over the five-year period. Finally, the analysis includes the same cyclical measure for the real exchange rate.

Cyclical fluctuations matter for economic growth. As table B.20 in appendix B shows, the output gap and GDP volatility have the expected positive and negative impacts on transitory growth, respectively. Both are statistically significant.[5] By contrast, real exchange rate volatility does not exhibit a statistically significant effect, possibly reflecting that some degree of exchange rate volatility is a welcome macroeconomic shock absorber, while only large swings in the exchange rate are a sign of macroeconomic vulnerability and mismanagement. These findings add to the previous statement that stabilization policies do in fact matter (as seen from the unconditional model), although their impact often is mediated indirectly through structural factors. The results from table B.20 further highlight that countries that are off their potential output trajectory revert to their longer-run growth rate, but that such deviations from potential output are harmful to long-run growth.

However, the key results from the baseline model are not significantly altered. Comparison of the other parameter estimates from table B.20 in appendix B with the baseline model in table 3.3 (in chapter 3) shows that the key results remain largely unaffected, although some of their magnitudes change. For example, the parameters for external factors and government consumption become smaller (in absolute values). In addition, the persistence term becomes smaller, which is perfectly in line with theory: in the growth equation representation (equation 3.2 in chapter 3), the income persistence term becomes a growth reversion term, which should pick up some degree of the "cyclical reversion" variable. Finally, the effect of the exchange rate becomes statistically significant, whereas financial development (as measured by credit/GDP) is no longer significant.

Alternative Measures of Infrastructure

The main reason for using telephone lines as the baseline proxy measure for telecommunications is that mobile phones were not widely used until the 1990s. The data set used in this report covers the period 1970–2010, so the analysis needs to use a proxy for telecommunications infrastructure that is relevant for the entire period.

However, there are some clear limitations to using this proxy alone, highlighting the need for additional robustness tests. First, the explosion in the use of mobile phones has limited the usefulness of landlines as a proxy for infrastructure. Not only are countries demanding more cell phones, but also they are replacing fixed lines with mobile phones.[6] Furthermore, considering other infrastructure sectors, such as roads, would reduce the potential upward bias of the contribution of infrastructure that takes place by including only landlines in the regression analysis. Finally, the inclusion of more than one infrastructure sector would result in different gaps in the different infrastructure sectors. Since telecommunications is the only sector that has improved dramatically since the opening of the sector, and is the only sector that has narrowed the gap vis-à-vis high-income countries, using it as the sole proxy may underestimate the infrastructure bottlenecks observed in LAC countries.

A first robustness test is run where transportation infrastructure replaces telecommunications. Columns 2 and 3 in table B.6 in appendix B show that transportation infrastructure, as captured by roads and railway lines per capita, also has a significant positive effect on GDP per capita growth.

The second robustness check considers more than one sector as a proxy for infrastructure. Following Calderón, Moral-Benito, and Servén (2014), a composite infrastructure index is used, comprising roads, telephone lines, and power generation capacity. The composite infrastructure index is constructed as follows: 0.36*ln(telephone lines per worker) + 0.35*ln(power generation capacity per worker) + 0.29*ln(road networks per worker). Table B.17 in appendix B reports estimates from regressions that are identical to those in table 3.3 (in chapter 3), except that telephone lines are replaced with the composite infrastructure index. The findings show that (i) the estimated elasticity coefficient on the composite infrastructure index is around 0.08, and thus positive and significantly different from zero at the 1 percent level; and (ii) the coefficients on the other variables change little relative to those in table 3.3. In the system–general method of moments (system-GMM) estimation reported in column 1 in table B.17, the Hansen J-statistic p-value is less than 0.05, but this p-value would be greater than 0.1 if an additional lag of GDP was included in the model, with little effect on the other coefficients.

While these results confirm the importance of closing the LAC region's infrastructure gap for productivity and growth, they also highlight serious data deficiencies. There are not enough good quality, internationally comparable data on infrastructure to allow for a more accurate picture of the needs and gaps. This situation underscores the need for a comprehensive effort to address data limitations as a key item in the development policy agenda going forward.

Notes

1. The interactions are instrumented by the instruments used for the linear model multiplied by the LAC dummy. Interactions were used (rather than splitting the sample) because this is more efficient; that is, there are more observations. There is also very little evidence of a significant difference in marginal effects for Caribbean countries (table B.11 in appendix B).

2. The country-specific coefficients are similar to those obtained from the restricted panel. In the panel literature (see, for example, Durlauf, Johnson, and Temple 2005), an important issue is whether cross-country parameter heterogeneity leads to a bias in the estimated average marginal effect in the restricted panel model. To explore this, the study estimated a panel model allowing for country-specific slope coefficients. The model was estimated on a balanced panel so that T = 8 for all countries. Each of the policy variables was included on the right-hand side one at a time, as this is the only feasible way to estimate the model given the data at hand. Figure B.1 in appendix B shows a kernel density plot and a histogram of the country-specific coefficients for each of the relevant policy variables of interest. Table B.12 in appendix B reports the estimated coefficients and their standard errors for each country in the sample. The important result is that the means (medians) of the country-specific coefficients (reported in the bottom right-hand side of table B.12) are quantitatively close to and not statistically different from the coefficients obtained in the restricted panel model; see table B.3 in appendix B for comparison.

3. See, for example, Ramey and Ramey (1995), Hnatkovska and Loayza (2005), Kose, Prasad, and Terrones (2006), and Crespo-Cuaresma, Klasen, and Wacker (2013).

4. See Ball (2014) for the long-run effects of the financial crisis, and Woodford (2009) for a discussion of the new macroeconomic synthesis. The issue of bringing the short and long runs together in neoclassical growth theory was raised by Solow (2005).

5. GDP volatility is positive and insignificant in the fixed effects model, which is not surprising, because it is endogenous to growth swings.

6. However, the number of observations for telephone lines is almost twice as large as for mobile phones. Hence, from an econometric point of view, telephone lines are a preferable proxy for telecommunications infrastructure. Therefore, a robustness check using mobile phones is not performed.

References

Alfaro, L., A. Chanda, S. Kalemli-Ozcan, and S. Sayek. 2004. "FDI and Economic Growth: The Role of Local Financial Markets." *Journal of International Economics* 64: 113–34.

Ball, Laurence. 2014. "Long-Term Damage from the Great Recession in OECD Countries." NBER Working Paper 20185, National Bureau of Economic Research, Cambridge, MA.

Borensztein E., J. De Gregorio, and J-W. Lee. 1998. "How Does Foreign Direct Investment Affect Economic Growth?" *Journal of International Economics* 45: 115–35.

Calderón, C., E. Moral-Benito, and L. Servén. 2014. "Is Infrastructure Capital Productive? A Dynamic Heterogeneous Approach." *Journal of Applied Econometrics*. Wiley Online Library. https://www.researchgate.net/publication/228304212_Is_Infrastructure_Capital_Productive_A_Dynamic_Heterogeneous_Approach.

Chang, R., L. Kaltani, and N. Loayza. 2009. "Openness Can Be Good for Growth: The Role of Policy Complementarities." *Journal of Development Economics* 90 (1): 33–49.

Crespo-Cuaresma, Jesús, Stephan Klasen, and Konstantin M. Wacker. 2013. "Why We Don't See Poverty Convergence: The Role of Macroeconomic Volatility." CRC Discussion Paper 153, Courant Research Center, Göttingen, Germany.

Durlauf, S., P. Johnson, and J. Temple. 2005. "Growth Econometrics." In *Handbook of Economic Growth*, edited by Philippe Aghion and Stefen Durlauf. Amsterdam, Netherlands: North-Holland.

Gallego, F., and N. Loayza. 2002. "The Golden Period for Growth in Chile: Explanations and Forecasts." In *Economic Growth: Sources, Trends, and Cycles*, Edited by N. Loayza and R. Soto. Santiago, Chile: Central Bank of Chile.

Hnatkovska, Viktoria, and Norman Loayza. 2005. "Volatility and Growth." In *Managing Economic Volatility and Crises: A Practitioner's Guide*, edited by Joshua Aizenman and Brian Pinto, 65–100. Cambridge, UK: Cambridge University Press.

Klein, M. W., and G. P. Olivei. 2008. "Capital Account Liberalization, Financial Depth, and Economic Growth." *Journal of International Money and Finance* 27 (6): 861–75.

Kose, Ayhan M., Eswar S. Prasad, and Marco E. Terrones. 2006. "How Do Trade and Financial Integration Affect the Relationship between Growth and Volatility?" *Journal of International Economics* 69 (1): 176–202.

Ramey, Garey, and Valerie A. Ramey. 1995. "Cross-Country Evidence on the Link between Volatility and Growth." *American Economic Review* 85 (5): 1138–51.

Solow, Robert M. 2005. "Reflections on Growth Theory." In *Handbook of Economic Growth*, edited by Philippe Aghion and Stefen Durlauf, 3–10. Amsterdam, Netherlands: North-Holland Elsevier.

Woodford, Michael. 2009. "Convergence in Macroeconomics: Elements of the New Synthesis." *American Economic Journal: Macroeconomics* 1 (1): 267–79.

7

What Might the Future Hold for LAC?

Trends from the Past Decade

This chapter focuses on estimating growth for the Latin America and the Caribbean (LAC) region for the 2010s, assuming that recent developments in the determinants of growth extend into the future. The spirit of the chapter is not to attempt to make projections about the future, but rather to extrapolate the trends identified by the model to the subsequent decade. Thus, this exercise should be understood as a form of sensitivity analysis, and help in understanding the economic implications of the econometric model discussed in chapter 3.

Country-by-country time-series regressions are used to generate growth predictions. The predictions are generated using the estimates in column 1 in table 3.3 (in chapter 3), and an AR(1) forecast is used to obtain future values of the explanatory variables. Because T = 8, this parsimonious model is estimated and used to compute the predicted change in each variable over two periods, 2011–15 and 2016–20.[1] Table B.13 in appendix B presents the growth forecasts for the countries in LAC in the sample. The first column shows the change in log gross domestic product (GDP) per capita between 2001 and 2010, and the second column shows the predicted change for 2011–20. The remaining columns in the table show how this predicted change is decomposed into persistence of GDP per capita growth and predicted changes in structural policies, stabilization policies, and the terms of trade. The comparison of predicted growth for the next decade (2011–20) with the previous decade (2001–10) is facilitated by figures 7.1 and 7.2. The figures show the predicted change in log GDP per capita during 2011–20 and the change in log GDP per capita during 2001–10 for countries located in South America, and Central America and the Caribbean, respectively.

FIGURE 7.1: Growth Predictions for South America under a Scenario of Continuous Trends

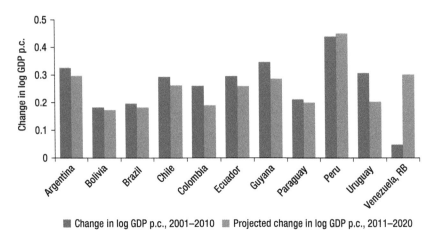

Note: GDP = gross domestic product; p.c. = per capita.

FIGURE 7.2: Growth Predictions for Central America and the Caribbean under a Scenario of Continuous Trends

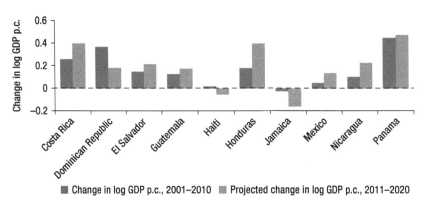

Note: GDP = gross domestic product; p.c. = per capita.

The model predicts that, extrapolating current trends, the average country in LAC would grow slightly faster in the second decade of this century than in the first. On average, the forecasts predict that countries in the region will expand during the 2010s by around 0.23 log points, or 2.3 percent per year. This is slightly higher than the expansion in the previous decade, which was around 0.22 log points. For countries located in South America, the forecasts predict an expansion of around 2.6 percent per year, slightly down by 0.1 percentage points from the expansion in the 2000s. The model predicts a modest increase in GDP per capita growth for countries in Central America and the Caribbean, up by 0.3 percentage points from 1.7 percent during 2001–10, to 2.0 percent during 2011–20. Table 7.1 summarizes the main findings.

The countries in the LAC region with the highest growth predictions are Panama, Peru, Costa Rica, and Honduras. Real purchasing power parity (PPP) GDP per capita is predicted to grow in these countries by 4.7, 4.5, 4.0, and 4.0 percent, respectively. For all four of these countries, the predictions for GDP per capita growth during 2011–20 are higher than the GDP per capita growth in the previous decade. More precisely, the predictions suggest an increase in the GDP per capita growth rate by 0.2 percentage points per year for Panama, 0.1 percentage points for Peru, 1.4 percentage points for Costa Rica, and 2.2 percentage points for Honduras. For Panama, 2.7 percentage points in annual GDP per capita growth during 2010–20 is predicted to be due to persistence, a quite substantial magnitude. Similarly, for Peru, Costa Rica, and Honduras, these numbers amount to 2.7, 1.1, and 1.6 percentage points, respectively. The predicted contributions from structural reforms are 2.1 percentage points for Panama, 1.6 percentage points for Peru, 2.4 percentage points for Costa Rica, and 2.8 percentage points for Honduras. The predicted growth contributions of stabilization policies and external conditions are minuscule for these countries, except for Peru where deteriorations in stabilization policies are expected to shave 0.2 percentage points of growth, while favorable external conditions are predicted to increase annual GDP per capita growth by 0.4 percentage points.

There are only two countries for which the model predicts negative GDP per capita growth: Haiti and Jamaica. Both of these countries are part of the Central American and Caribbean region. For Haiti, the forecasts predict a negative change in real PPP GDP per capita during 2011–20 of around −0.06 log points, or −0.6 percent per year, thus down by nearly 0.7 percentage points per year relative to the expansion of the previous decade. For Jamaica, the predicted drop in GDP per capita growth is even larger: real PPP GDP per capita is estimated to decrease during 2011–20 by around −0.16 log points, equivalent to a negative GDP per capita growth rate of −1.6 percentage points. For Haiti, 0.1 percentage points in annual GDP per capita growth during 2010–20 is predicted to be due to persistence; for Jamaica this number amounts

TABLE 7.1: **Summary of Model Predictions If Trends from the Past Decade Persisted into the Future**

Highest growth predictions	Predictions of negative growth	Strongest predicted growth accelerations	Strongest predicted growth decelerations
Costa Rica	Haiti	Costa Rica	Dominican Republic
Honduras	Jamaica	Honduras	Jamaica
Panama		Nicaragua	Uruguay
Peru		República Bolivariana de Venezuela	

to −0.2 percentage points. The predicted contributions from structural reforms are −0.4 percentage points for Haiti and −1.2 percentage points for Jamaica. The predicted growth contributions arising from stabilization policies are −0.1 percentage points for Haiti and −0.2 percentage points for Jamaica. Deteriorations in external conditions are expected to shave 0.1 and 0.2 percentage points of annual GDP per capita growth in Jamaica and Haiti, respectively.

The countries for which the model predicts the strongest acceleration in GDP per capita growth are Costa Rica and Nicaragua, and, perhaps surprisingly, Honduras and República Bolivariana de Venezuela. República Bolivariana de Venezuela's GDP per capita growth rate is predicted to increase by around 2.5 percentage points, from 0.5 percent during 2001–10 to 3.0 percent during 2011–20; Honduras's GDP per capita growth rate is predicted to increase by around 2.2 percentage points, from 1.8 percent during 2001–10 to 4.0 percent during 2011–20; Costa Rica's GDP per capita growth rate is predicted to increase by around 1.4 percentage points, from 2.6 percent during 2001–10 to 4.0 percent during 2011–20; and Nicaragua's GDP per capita growth rate is predicted to increase by around 1.3 percentage points, from 1.0 percent during 2001–10 to 2.3 percent during 2011–20.

For Nicaragua, 0.6 percentage points in annual GDP per capita growth during 2010–20 is predicted to be due to persistence; for Costa Rica, Honduras, and República Bolivariana de Venezuela, these numbers amount to 1.6, 1.1, and 0.3 percentage points, respectively. The predicted contributions from structural reforms are 1.4 percentage points for Nicaragua, 2.4 percentage points for Costa Rica, 2.8 percentage points for Honduras, and 2.7 percentage points for República Bolivariana de Venezuela. The predicted growth contributions arising from changes in stabilization policies and external conditions are minuscule, except for Nicaragua and República Bolivariana de Venezuela, where improvements in external conditions are predicted to add to GDP per capita growth by around 0.1 and 0.2 percentage points, respectively. Deteriorations (improvements) in stabilization policies in República Bolivariana de Venezuela (Nicaragua) are expected to shave 0.2 (add 0.1) percentage points of (to) annual GDP per capita growth.

The countries for which the forecasts predict the strongest deceleration in GDP per capita growth (by over 1 percentage points per year) are the Dominican Republic, Jamaica, and Uruguay. The Dominican Republic's GDP per capita growth rate is predicted to decrease by around 1.9 percentage points per year, from 3.7 percent during 2001–10 to 1.8 percent during 2011–20; Jamaica's GDP per capita growth rate is predicted to decrease by around 1.4 percentage points per year, from −0.2 percent during 2001–10 to −1.6 percent during 2011–20; and Uruguay's GDP per capita growth rate is predicted to decrease by around 1.1 percentage points per year, from 3.1 percent during 2001–10 to 2.0 percent during 2011–20.

For the Dominican Republic, 2.2 percentage points in annual GDP per capita growth during 2010–20 are predicted to be due to persistence; for Jamaica and Uruguay, these numbers amount to −0.2 and 1.9 percentage points, respectively.

The predicted contributions from structural reforms are −0.5 percentage points for the Dominican Republic, −1.2 percentage points for Jamaica, and 0.2 percentage points for Uruguay. The predicted growth contributions arising from changes in stabilization policies and external conditions are minuscule, except for Jamaica, where deteriorations in external conditions are expected to shave 0.2 percentage points of annual GDP per capita growth.

The proxy for infrastructure that is chosen matters for the aggregate and individual country results. For Honduras and República Bolivariana de Venezuela, the most important contributor to the positive growth forecast is telecommunications. During the past decade, both countries experienced a significant expansion in telecommunications infrastructure. The model's projection is that this trend will continue and thus contribute positively to growth, about 2 percent per year. In contrast, the model projects that in these countries developments in transportation infrastructure instead of telecommunications would only have a minuscule effect on economic growth, as shown in table B.14 in appendix B. Therefore, replacing telecommunications with roads would remove Honduras and República Bolivariana de Venezuela from the group of countries with the highest forecast rates of growth acceleration. Overall, for the growth forecasts (2011–20), the main contribution to economic growth comes from continued expansion in the telecommunications sector; there is little contribution coming from transportation infrastructure. This result can be seen by comparing table B.13 with table B.14.

The growth forecasts based on the composite infrastructure index (using the estimates in column 1 in table B.16 in appendix B) yield results that are similar to the baseline specification. Table B.16 shows that the mean (10-year) growth forecast contribution from the composite infrastructure index for LAC is around 0.059; this is very close to the number presented in table B.14 in appendix B, based on telecommunications only, which is 0.058. However, there are differences at the individual country level. For some countries, the contribution from the composite infrastructure index is lower relative to using telecommunications, while for other countries the opposite is the case.

These results highlight the challenges to growth going forward. The previous analysis showed that the influence of stabilization policies has approached a threshold plateau where further growth-promoting effects from additional improvements in macro policy making become more difficult to achieve. Similarly, doing "more of the same," for example, in public infrastructure provisioning, is unlikely to drive growth in the future. Instead, governments in LAC should find ways to identify the most pressing infrastructure bottlenecks in the future and provide them in an efficient manner. Furthermore, table 7.1 highlights that a considerable fraction of predicted growth stems from persistence, that is, a certain level of path dependence. The obtained predictions should thus not leave policy makers too confident about the future of growth, but should alert them to the need to identify new sources of growth by addressing the most pressing domestic bottlenecks.

Commodity Prices

Another way to gauge the importance of the external environment is to examine its impact on growth forecasts in a situation where the external environment ceases to improve. Therefore, forecasts for growth in 2011–20 are conducted under a scenario of continuous AR(1) trends for all variables *except* the commodity price index and the terms of trade. The latter are assumed to remain at their 2010 levels, which is the definition of cessation of improvement adopted here. This exercise is broadly consistent with the approach followed by Talvi and Munyo (2013), who look into the relationship between the External Conditions Index and the LAC-7 growth rate.[2,3]

This exercise does not significantly change the baseline forecasts, except for some of the LAC commodity exporters. As shown in table B.18 in appendix B, for the LAC region as a whole, the predicted growth forecast is around 2.2 percent, compared with 2.3 percent in table B.14. For some countries, most notably the commodity-exporting countries, the difference is somewhat more significant. For example, when keeping external conditions at their 2010 values, Chile's growth forecast declines by around 0.6 percentage points (to 2.0 percent); Peru's growth forecast declines by around 0.4 percentage points (to 4.1 percent); and República Bolivariana de Venezuela's growth forecast declines by around 0.2 percentage points (to 2.8 percent).

In view of the ongoing decline in commodity prices, it seems appropriate to analyze growth trends under a scenario of adverse external trends. This is done by modeling a scenario for the 2010s where the growth rates of the international commodity price index and the terms of trade index are just equal to the negative of the growth rates of these variables for the 2000s. The projections for structural policies, stabilization policies, and persistence remain the same. These results are reported in table B.19 in appendix B. As expected, a reversal in international commodity prices would have an adverse impact on the growth prospects of commodity-exporting countries, even if trends in other growth drivers persisted. For the LAC region as a whole, the predicted growth forecast is around 1.6 percent, again compared with 2.3 percent in table B.14. The most severely impacted countries in this exercise, according to the model's predictions, would be Chile and República Bolivariana de Venezuela, with growth forecasts moving to slightly negative terrain. In the case of República Bolivariana de Venezuela, in particular, the growth acceleration that would be expected under a continuous trends scenario for all variables would simply vanish. Peru's growth performance would also slow down as a result: its growth forecast declines by around 1.2 percentage points (to 3.3 percent).

Benchmarking Exercise on the Effects of Changes in Structural and Stabilization Features

Identifying the performance of LAC countries in structural and stabilization policies is important for locating the areas in which the most binding constraints to growth may lie.

Looking at five years of the sample (2005–10), some countries in LAC had good performance in their structural and stabilization policies. Figure 7.3 shows a scatter plot of a structural policy index and a stabilization policy index. The scatter plot identifies whether structural or stabilization policies, or both types of policies, posed large binding constraints for GDP per capita growth. The structural policy index is constructed for each country in LAC by taking the log-levels of the structural policy variables (financial development, education, political institutions, trade openness, infrastructure, and government size) in 2005–10 and multiplying them by their respective unconditional effects coefficients.[4] These values are then added together and the resulting distribution for LAC is normalized to the [0, 1] space.[5] This process ranks each country's structural policy performance using the log-level of each variable and its contribution to the level of GDP per capita (evidenced by the unconditional effects coefficients) with respect to the rest of the countries in LAC. The same is done for the stabilization policy index using the stabilization policy variables (inflation, real exchange rate, and banking crisis).

It is important to stress that the benchmarking exercise is intended as a first approximation to sequencing and prioritization of reforms, a kind of *triage*, rather than a full diagnostic. That is, the exercise is an entry point for more in-depth

FIGURE 7.3: **Structural Policy and Stabilization Policy Indexes, 2005–10**

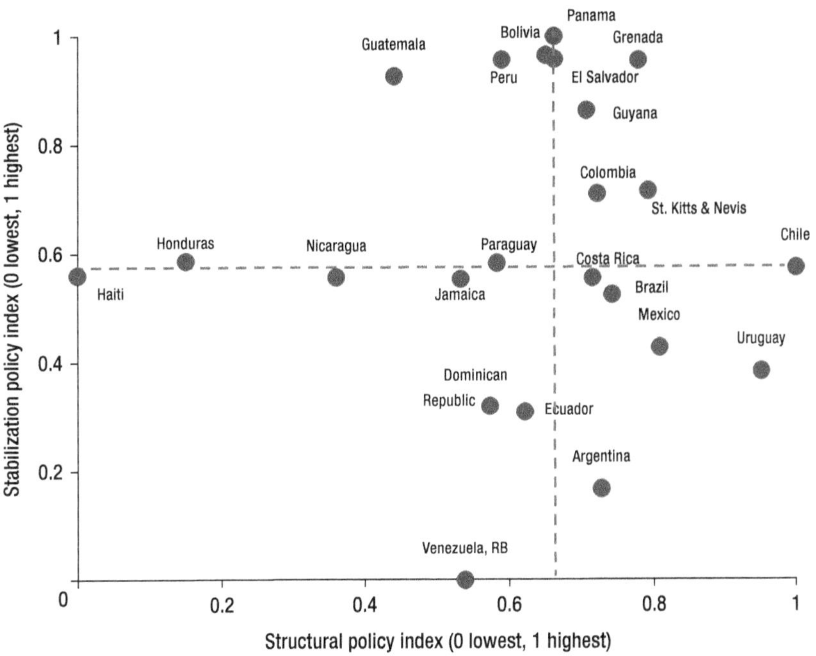

Source: World Bank Group staff calculations based on Brueckner 2014.

country analysis. In this vein, it should be interpreted as a *thought experiment*—the feasibility of such reforms would need to be determined by a country-specific assessment of implementation capacity, the economic costs of each of the reforms, and political economy issues, which is beyond the scope of this study. Therefore, the goal of the exercise is to identify the structural and stabilization features that matter the most for each country vis-à-vis a chosen benchmark, rather than providing fully realistic simulations of policy changes. Furthermore, although it is indeed unrealistic that countries will close the largest gaps, it seems reasonable to assume that any progress will most easily be made by policies concerning large existing gaps and the associated "low-hanging fruits" compared with gaps where countries are close to the frontier.

There is no country that was a top performer in both structural and stabilization policies, suggesting that there is room for growth gains from policy changes in the region. The scatter plot in figure 7.3 shows which countries were among the top performers in the two categories of policies (the dotted red lines depict the median of each policy index). If a country was a top performer in both stabilization and structural policies, it would be located at coordinates (1, 1); conversely, if it was a bottom performer in both types of policies, it would be located at the origin. The indexes were normalized to the [0, 1] space among the LAC distribution of countries. The further away from the origin a country is, the fewer binding constraints to growth it potentially has.

Chile and Uruguay emerge as the top performers in structural policies, and Honduras and Haiti as the bottom performers, meaning that the largest binding constraints for the latter two countries are potentially among the structural policy variables. For stabilization policies, Bolivia and Panama are the top performers, and Argentina and República Bolivariana de Venezuela are the bottom performers, suggesting that the largest binding constraints for the latter two countries are potentially among stabilization policy variables. Countries that do not appear to have been largely constrained by either type of policy are in the first quadrant (Chile, Colombia, Grenada, Guyana, Panama, and St. Kitts and Nevis). It is important to note that these policy indexes are calculated with respect to the LAC region and give a sense of the policy areas from which growth benefited the most.[6]

This benchmarking exercise looks into the counterfactual per capita income a country would have achieved if it were a top performer for each explanatory variable. The exercise will help to determine the possible effects that a stellar performance (relative to the rest of LAC) in specific policy areas might have had for a country's level of GDP per capita. The benchmarking exercise is performed by looking at the LAC countries' distribution for each of the variables included in the model (those that fall under the structural and stabilization policy categories) and taking the log-level of the country at the 90th percentile of the distribution.[7] That log-level is then multiplied by the unconditional effects coefficient to obtain the effects on a counterfactual GDP per capita. This in turn allows comparison of the actual level of GDP per capita for a specific country against the counterfactual level of GDP per capita of setting a certain variable at the level of a top-performing economy in LAC.

The exercise provides an indication of the possible gains in the GDP per capita level that a country would have had if it had been a top performer in a specific area. It is important to highlight that the analysis uses unconditional effects coefficients, as they capture the overall within-country effect that a variable (for example, schooling or financial development) has on GDP per capita. Furthermore, the approach is an inspection similar to a triage that tries to prioritize policy areas quickly based on the severity of their actual conditions. This cross-country process has to neglect country-specific characteristic and data issues; therefore, the results should not be interpreted mechanically. The results serve as a starting point to think about policy prioritization. Appendix A discusses the benchmarking methodology in greater detail.

Stabilization Policy Benchmarking

Countries such as Argentina, the Dominican Republic, Ecuador, and República Bolivariana de Venezuela would have seen the greatest increase in percentage terms in the level of GDP per capita if their performance in inflation had been at the level of the top performers in LAC. Figure 7.4 shows the actual and counterfactual levels of GDP per capita of a better performance in inflation. The green dots in the figure

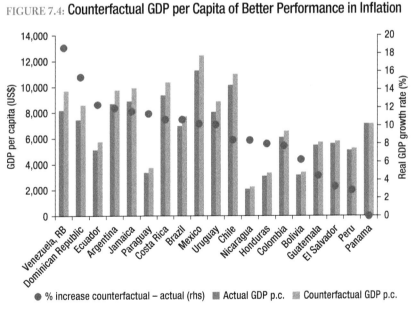

FIGURE 7.4: **Counterfactual GDP per Capita of Better Performance in Inflation**

● % increase counterfactual – actual (rhs)   ■ Actual GDP p.c.   ▨ Counterfactual GDP p.c.

Source: World Bank Group staff calculations based on Brueckner 2014.
Note: GDP = gross domestic product; p.c. = per capita; rhs = right-hand side.

represent the percentage difference between the counterfactual and actual GDP per capita, and can be seen as what a country potentially stands to gain by enhancing its performance in inflation. República Bolivariana de Venezuela would have seen an 18 percent increase in its level of GDP per capita if its inflation had been at the level of that in Panama (the 93rd percentile performer). Argentina would have seen an increase of 12 percent in its level of GDP per capita. Among countries in LAC, these two countries stand to gain the most from an improvement in inflation management.

Mexico, Panama, and República Bolivariana de Venezuela would have seen substantial increases in the level of GDP per capita if their performance in real exchange rate management had been at the level of the top performers in LAC. Figure 7.5 shows the actual and counterfactual levels of GDP per capita with a better performance in real exchange rate management. República Bolivariana de Venezuela would have seen a 5 percent increase in its level of GDP per capita if its real exchange rate management had been at the level of Paraguay (the 93rd percentile performer). Mexico also would have seen an increase of 5 percent in its level of GDP per capita. Among countries in LAC, these two countries stand to gain the most from an enhancement of real exchange rate management. The result stands out that Panama is the third country that would benefit the most from an enhancement in real exchange rate management, as the country was ranked among the top performers in the overall stabilization policy index. Panama had an adequate

FIGURE 7.5: **Counterfactual GDP per Capita of Better Performance in Real Exchange Rate Management**

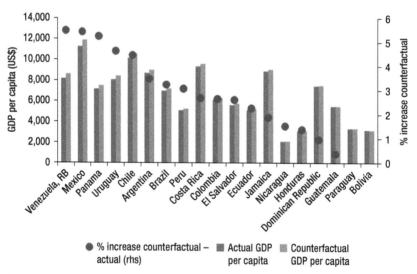

Source: World Bank Group staff calculations based on Brueckner 2014.
Note: GDP = gross domestic product; rhs = right-hand side.

performance in inflation management, as evidenced in the previous paragraph, but a very poor performance in real exchange rate management.

Structural Policy Benchmarking

El Salvador and Guatemala would have benefited the most in potential increases in GDP per capita if their performance in education had been at the level of the top performers in LAC. Figure 7.6 shows the actual and counterfactual levels of GDP per capita with more years of schooling as a proxy for performance in education. El Salvador and Guatemala would have had the largest percentage increase in GDP per capita within LAC countries if their level of years of schooling had been that of Brazil (the 92nd percentile performer).[8] El Salvador and Guatemala would have seen increases of 3 and 5 percent, respectively, in their level of GDP per capita.

Argentina and República Bolivariana de Venezuela would have benefited the most in potential increases in GDP per capita if their performance in financial development, as measured by credit to the private sector over GDP, had been at the level of the top performers in LAC. Figure 7.7 shows the actual and counterfactual levels of GDP per capita with higher levels of credit to GDP. Argentina and República Bolivariana de Venezuela would have had the largest percentage increase

FIGURE 7.6: **Counterfactual GDP per Capita of Better Performance in Education**

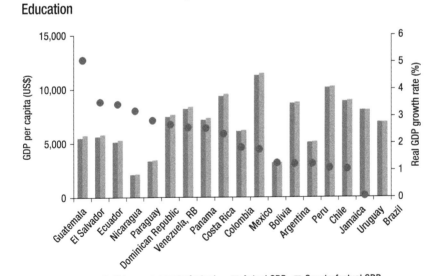

Source: World Bank Group staff calculations based on Brueckner 2014.
Note: GDP = gross domestic product; rhs = right-hand side.

FIGURE 7.7: Counterfactual GDP per Capita of Better Performance in Financial Development

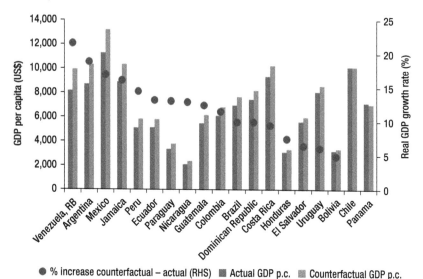

● % increase counterfactual – actual (RHS) ■ Actual GDP p.c. ▨ Counterfactual GDP p.c.

Source: World Bank Group calculations based on Brueckner 2014.
Note: GDP = gross domestic product; p.c. = per capita; RHS = right-hand side.

in GDP per capita within LAC countries if their level of credit over GDP had been that of Chile (the 92nd percentile performer). Argentina and República Bolivariana de Venezuela would have seen increases of 19 and 22 percent, respectively, in their level of GDP per capita. República Bolivariana de Venezuela, with an increase of 22 percent from its actual to its counterfactual GDP per capita level, is the country that stands to gain the most from an enhancement of any type of policy variable included in the model.

Honduras, Nicaragua, and Paraguay would have seen the largest increases in percentage terms in the level of GDP per capita if their performance in infrastructure had been at the level of the top performers in LAC. Figure 7.8 shows the actual and counterfactual levels of GDP per capita of a better performance in infrastructure equivalent to the top performers. Nicaragua would have seen an increase of 19 percent in its level of GDP per capita, and Paraguay 15 percent if the level of infrastructure, as measured by number of main telephone lines per capita, had been the same as that of Grenada (the 92nd percentile performer). It is interesting to note that, in the case of this particular measure of infrastructure, a country's gap with respect to the top performer shows a fairly clear inverse correlation with its per capita income level.

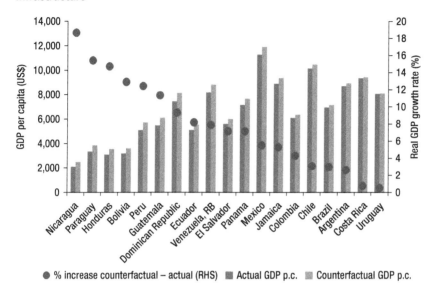

● % increase counterfactual – actual (RHS)   ■ Actual GDP p.c.   ▦ Counterfactual GDP p.c.

Source: World Bank Group staff calculations based on Brueckner 2014.
Note: GDP = gross domestic product; p.c. = per capita; rhs = right-hand side.

Honduras and Panama would have seen the largest increases in percentage terms in the level of GDP per capita if their level of goods trade had been at the level of the top performers in LAC. Figure 7.9 shows the actual and counterfactual levels of GDP per capita of a better performance in trade openness, equivalent to the top performers in the region. Panama would have seen an increase of 16 percent in its level of GDP per capita. However, this result comes with a grain of salt, as it is based on goods trade and conditional on the size of the population. Honduras would have experienced an increase in per capita GDP of 14 percent if its level of trade openness, as measured by exports plus imports over GDP, had been at the level of that in Uruguay (the 92nd percentile performer).

Honduras and Nicaragua would have seen the largest increases in percentage terms in the level of GDP per capita if their level of government size had been at the level of the top performers in LAC. Figure 7.10 shows the actual and counterfactual levels of GDP per capita with better performance in government size, equivalent to the top performers in the region. Nicaragua would have seen an increase of 15 percent in its level of GDP per capita and Honduras 14 percent, if their level of government size, as measured by government consumption over GDP, had been as low as that of República Bolivariana de Venezuela (the 92nd percentile performer).

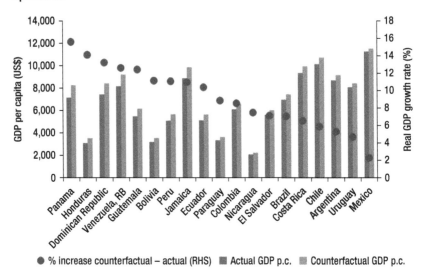

FIGURE 7.9: Counterfactual GDP per Capita of Better Performance in Trade Openness

● % increase counterfactual – actual (RHS)　■ Actual GDP p.c.　▨ Counterfactual GDP p.c.

Source: World Bank Group calculations based on Brueckner 2014.
Note: GDP = gross domestic product; p.c. = per capita; RHS = right-hand side.

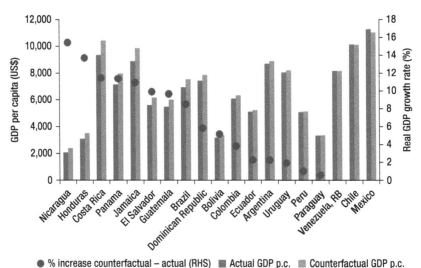

FIGURE 7.10: Counterfactual GDP per Capita of Better Performance in Government Size

● % increase counterfactual – actual (RHS)　■ Actual GDP p.c.　▨ Counterfactual GDP p.c.

Source: World Bank Group staff calculations based on Brueckner 2014.
Note: GDP = gross domestic product; p.c. = per capita; RHS = right-hand side.

Notes

1. Forecasts were also computed with richer time-series models that include linear and quadratic trends. The results were similar to the ones reported here. Estimation of ARMA-type models was not feasible, because for the majority of the variables and countries the maximum likelihood estimator did not achieve convergence.

2. The External Conditions Index is a weighted average of global economic growth, commodity prices, and international financial conditions (as proxied by Emerging Market Bond Index spreads). LAC-7 is the simple average of the GDPs of Argentina, Brazil, Chile, Colombia, Mexico, Peru, and República Bolivariana de Venezuela.

3. Talvi and Munyo (2013, 11) attribute the ongoing growth slowdown among the LAC-7 to stagnating—albeit still favorable—external conditions: "Therefore, the cooling-off that LAC-7 is currently experiencing is the natural and predictable outcome of external conditions which remain favorable for the region—even more favorable on average than those of the Golden Years, *but that have ceased to improve*" (emphasis added).

4. These unconditional effects are the ones found in table 3.3 (in chapter 3) and are not country specific. This approach again takes a "Thinking Big" macro perspective, in the sense that it abstracts from the questions of how the effects might operate and through which particular policies and interventions reforms might be implemented. This is not to say that those questions would not be highly relevant, but they are beyond the scope of this study and left to future investigations.

5. For Haiti and Honduras, data for the education variable (years of schooling) are not available for 2005–10. The lack of availability of schooling data is not penalized, as the structural policy index is constructed by taking the sum of the multiplication of the log-level of each variable and the unconditional effect coefficient and dividing it by the sum of the coefficients for which data are available for 2005–10 for each country case.

6. The reasoning behind this is that LAC had a sound performance in GDP per capita growth in the past decade compared with other regions of the world (as evidenced in chapter 2). Hence, a within-region comparison is appropriate to identify adequate performance in certain policy areas and potential binding constraints in other policy areas.

7. For certain variables a country in the exact 90th percentile in the distribution is not available, as the number of countries is limited to those in LAC. In these cases, the analysis uses the country falling within the 90th to 93rd percentile range.

8. Since schooling data for Haiti and Honduras are not available for 2005–10, these countries were not included in this benchmarking exercise.

References

Brueckner, M. 2014. Background paper for this report. Mimeo. World Bank Group, Washington, DC.

Talvi, E., and I. Munyo. 2013. "Latin America Macroeconomic Outlook: A Global Perspective. Are the Golden Years for Latin America Over?" Brookings-CERES Macroeconomic Report. Brookings Institution, Washington, DC.

8

What Do the Findings Mean for the Policy Debate?

Drivers of Growth

The Growth Commission Report (Commission on Growth and Development 2008) opens its policy discussion with a rare acknowledgment: "We do not know the sufficient conditions for growth." Although it is possible to outline the main features of fast-growing economies, it is a much more difficult task to pin down the ultimate or fundamental factors behind growth performance. Based on the available evidence and country experience, the Growth Commission Report enumerates a broad list of ingredients for sustained growth, without attempting to transform the list into a growth strategy or advocating that all the elements in the list are necessary for growth. The chief ingredients on the list include (i) high levels of investment (in infrastructure, physical capital, and human capital); (ii) technology transfer; (iii) product market competition; (iv) well-functioning labor markets; (v) macroeconomic stability; (vi) financial sector development; (vii) equity and equality of opportunity; and (viii) effective government.

Although the findings from this study should not be mechanically translated into policy recommendations, they do reveal broad policy directions that could help to inform growth strategies in the region. First and foremost, the strategies that promoted growth in the past will not bring the region further. The drivers of growth in Latin America and the Caribbean (LAC) shifted somewhat over the past decade. Compared with previous studies on the subject, this study finds less evidence of the role of stabilization policies for growth in LAC. This finding probably reflects the fact that most of the countries in LAC already brought their macroeconomic house in order throughout the 1990s, which facilitated reaping benefits from other sources of growth in the period thereafter, but no longer constitutes a means of growth. Conversely, structural policies continued to play a key role in growth. But for many countries in LAC, most notably net commodity exporters, external conditions were an essential driver of growth over the past decade. This broad pattern suggests that some sources of growth can shift over time. External conditions might change in the future and are mostly beyond the region's control. Structural policies, such as those listed in the Growth Commission Report, are easier to shape and have turned out as a robust determinant of growth.

Benchmarking

The benchmarking exercise carried out in this study can help facilitate selectivity, sequencing, and prioritizing in the design of growth strategies. It does so by shedding light on where the "biggest bang for the buck" could be for countries in LAC, without attempting to identify the "ultimate" sources of growth. However, this exercise should be viewed as a first approximation. As such, it needs to be complemented by other sources of information—especially at the sector and microeconomic levels—to generate a more comprehensive picture of the main constraints to growth in individual countries in the region.

Benchmarking also reveals significant cross-country heterogeneity across the region. Better performance in stabilization-related features of the economy would have clearly benefited Argentina, Ecuador, and República Bolivariana de Venezuela, while having a significantly lower impact elsewhere in the region. The counterfactual impact of improved structural features varies widely across the region, where the main would-be beneficiaries are Guatemala (education), Nicaragua (infrastructure and government size), Panama (trade openness), and República Bolivariana de Venezuela (financial development). Thus, the Growth Commission Report's list is broadly reflected in the region's growth experience, *but different ingredients have different weights depending on the country.*

Sound Macro Policy

The relatively smaller role found for stabilization policies as a growth driver should not detract from the fact that a sound macro policy framework remains a prerequisite for sustained growth. Recent research has linked low total factor productivity growth in several countries in LAC to questionable policy choices over many years, including fiscal mismanagement and excessive state *dirigisme* in investment and production decisions.[1] An inadequate macroeconomic policy framework adversely affects private investment and growth by lowering the expected returns on investment projects and increasing the risk premium demanded by risk-averse investors to undertake a project (Montiel 2011). Some countries in the region are currently pursuing policies that fall squarely on the Growth Commission Report's "don't do" list, including excessive currency appreciation, energy subsidies, and import and forex restrictions Commission on Growth and Development (2008). Although such policies may provide a stopgap "solution" to short-term imbalances or address political pressures, they are not easily reversible and could adversely affect countries' ability to converge for years to come.

Maintaining a stable macroeconomic framework is all the more important in natural resource–rich countries, as indicated by the evidence for Argentina, Ecuador, and República Bolivariana de Venezuela. Natural resource–rich countries need to pay particular attention to commodity price volatility, real exchange rate overvaluation risks, and heightened potential for corruption and rent-seeking. An integrated approach to fiscal policy Medas and Zakharova (2009) in this context could be particularly useful to (i) reduce the costs of export and fiscal revenue volatility by de-linking government spending from short-term fluctuations on commodity prices; (ii) safeguard the quality of public spending through strengthened public financial management systems; (iii) ensure longer-term fiscal sustainability through the application of an appropriate sustainability benchmark, such as the permanent income model or other variants,[2] especially for oil exporters; and (iv) manage uncertainty, for example through the adoption of medium-term fiscal frameworks. At the same time, enhancing transparency in the management of revenues from natural resources is essential for the credibility of fiscal policy as well as for overall country governance.

The empirical findings also confirm the existence of a significant gap between infrastructure needs and investments, particularly for the poorer countries in the region. It is a well-known fact that LAC lags behind East Asian economies in infrastructure-related metrics such as electricity installed capacity and road density.[3] The counterfactual exercise conducted in chapter 7 suggests significant potential per capita income gains for countries at the lower end of the regional distribution of income, including Bolivia, Honduras, and Nicaragua. Paraguay, a lower-middle-income country, would also stand to gain considerably from infrastructure investments—a result that is consistent with previous work on the subject World Bank (2013). The results are also in line with other recent research on the contribution of infrastructure to aggregate output.[4]

Indirect effects of distinct policy levers may also matter for growth results. A case in point is the proxy for governance, or Polity2, which is found to have had a statistically insignificant impact on growth, despite the positive correlation between Polity2 and per capita gross domestic product (GDP) growth (as well as lagged per capita GDP), as reported in table 3.2 (in chapter 3). This finding is reminiscent of Loayza, Fajnzylber, and Calderón (2005), where the estimated coefficients of their governance index were also not statistically significant. They interpreted their results as meaning that "the effect of governance on economic growth works through the actual economic policies that governments implement" (Calderón, Moral-Benito, and Servén 2014, 56). This interpretation seems to be plausible in the present case as well, particularly given the positive correlation between Polity2 and other structural variables, such as schooling, credit, and infrastructure. That is, given this potential indirect effect, it cannot be concluded from the empirical analysis that governance is irrelevant for growth. Other indirect growth transmission mechanisms can be thought of as well. For example, human capital–augmenting education spending may affect growth directly and indirectly through, say, its positive impact on the profitability of private investments, which in turn could prompt increased availability of private credit.

Governments' Role

The empirical findings also provide a glimpse of the potential role of governments in facilitating growth.[5] On the one hand, government consumption has a negative impact on long-run growth to the extent that government consumption may be associated with the crowding-out of private investments (if it leads to higher interest rates through debt financing of the public deficit), distortions (such as high taxes), or inefficiencies (for example, a bloated public bureaucracy), without generating clear social returns. An important caveat is that higher government consumption embedded in fiscal stimulus may have a positive impact on output in the short term, as long as there is sufficient slackness and fiscal space in the economy. On the other hand, educational attainment and infrastructure services—which are at least partly funded by public sectors—would have a positive impact on growth. Therefore, *the composition of public spending matters for growth*: its impact will only be positive if it helps support the accumulation of human capital (through education) or physical capital (through infrastructure).[6,7] More broadly, governments can also facilitate growth by maintaining a stable and predictable policy environment, at the macro- and microeconomic levels.

Notes

1. See Soto and Zurita (2011), as well as the country case studies in the same issue of the journal. The emphasis that this new research places on policies as a main driver of total factor productivity growth contrasts to some extent with Easterly's (2005) point that robust associations between economic policy variables and growth occur for extreme values of the former.

2. See also Van Der Ploeg and Venables (2011).

3. See, for example, World Bank (2011, 26–27).

4. See, in particular, Calderón, Moral-Benito, and Servén (2014).

5. Given the high level of aggregation of the data used in the empirical analysis, this study does not provide much insight into the potential role of industrial or sector-specific policies.

6. It is also conceivable that government spending on education may positively affect growth through total factor productivity by means of human capital externalities.

7. In the short term, increases in government consumption—as part of a fiscal stimulus package— can have an impact on output during a cyclical downturn (and especially so in the context of the zero lower bound), depending on the size of the fiscal multiplier.

References

Calderón, C., E. Moral-Benito, and L. Servén. 2014. "Is Infrastructure Capital Productive? A Dynamic Heterogeneous Approach." *Journal of Applied Econometrics*. Published online in Wiley Online Library. https://www.researchgate.net/publication/228304212_Is_Infrastructure _Capital_Productive_A_Dynamic_Heterogeneous_Approach.

Commission on Growth and Development. 2008. *The Growth Report: Strategies for Sustained Growth and Inclusive Development*. Washington, DC: World Bank.

Easterly, W. 2005. "National Policies and Economic Growth: A Reappraisal." In *Handbook of Economic Growth*, volume 1A, edited by P. Aghion and S. N. Durlauf. Amsterdam, Netherlands: Elsevier.

Loayza, Norman, Pablo Fajnzylber, and César Calderón. 2005. *Economic Growth in Latin America and the Caribbean: Stylized Facts, Explanations, and Forecasts*. Washington, DC: World Bank Group.

Medas, P., and D. Zakharova. 2009. "A Primer on Fiscal Analysis in Oil-Producing Countries." IMF Working Paper WP/09/56, International Monetary Fund, Washington, DC.

Montiel, P. 2011. *Macroeconomics in Emerging Markets*. Second edition. Cambridge, UK: Cambridge University Press.

Polity IV. 2012. "Political Regime Characteristics and Transitions." Online Database. http://www .systemicpeace.org/polity/polity4.htm.

Soto, R., and F. Zurita. 2011. "Two Centuries of Economic Growth: Latin America at Its Bicentennial Celebration." *Latin American Journal of Economics* 48 (2): 113–32.

Van Der Ploeg, F., and A. Venables. 2011. "Harnessing Windfall Revenues: Optimal Policies for Resource-Rich Developing Economies." *Economic Journal* 121: 1–30.

World Bank. 2011. *Latin America and the Caribbean's Long-Term Growth: Made in China?* Washington, DC: LCR's Office of the Chief Economist, World Bank.

———. 2013. Paraguay Policy Notes. Unpublished report. World Bank, Washington, DC.

9
Conclusions

This study reevaluated the growth performance of Latin America and the Caribbean (LAC) based on new data for the first decade of the 21st century. This new information allowed for a reassessment of the respective roles of structural reforms, stabilization policies, and external conditions in the region's growth performance, taking the seminal contribution of Loayza, Fajnzylber, and Calderón (2005) as a starting point. In so doing, this study sheds additional light on a question that has been central to the development policy debate in the region: to what extent has growth been driven by external or domestic factors?

First, as expected, external conditions play a significant role in explaining LAC's growth performance, reflecting the commodity price boom and favorable terms of trade developments. An important fraction of growth during the 2000s in resource-rich countries can be explained by external conditions, as measured by time dummies to capture global shocks, terms-of-trade growth, and commodity price windfalls. For example, average growth of gross domestic product per capita in Chile, Guyana, and República Bolivariana de Venezuela during the 2000s was boosted by positive terms-of-trade developments by over 2 percentage points.

Second, stabilization policies played a less significant role than they did in earlier empirical assessments of growth performance. This finding may be because many countries in LAC managed to put their macroeconomic house in order during the 1990s and 2000s, thus reducing the importance of such policies as engines for promoting growth further. This result confirms the considerations of the relationship between inflation and growth in chapter 5. It should be stressed that this does not diminish the importance of macroeconomic stability as a *precondition* for growth.[1] It just means that the contribution of stabilization policies to growth became less pronounced, as many countries in LAC had already reaped the direct gains from stabilization in the late 1990s and early 2000s. Furthermore, stabilization policies potentially continued to support growth indirectly in the past decade, since a stable macroeconomic environment can help countries take advantage of favorable external conditions.[2]

Third, and perhaps more important, structural reforms continued to play a significant explanatory role, *even after controlling for the commodity boom*. Changes in structural policies had larger effects on the growth of countries in LAC than changes in stabilization policies. Moreover, LAC's recent growth performance cannot be reduced to the commodity boom. Financial development, trade openness, and infrastructure are confirmed to have been growth-enhancing, while government size has been shown to have been growth-reducing. However, political institutions are not statistically significant in the multivariate model.[3]

The main drivers of growth in LAC are not significantly different from those in other regions. External tailwinds were not significantly different for the LAC region. The same applies to the growth effects of structural policies and stabilization policies. From that standpoint, there seems to be nothing very particular about the drivers of growth in LAC relative to other regions.

Within LAC, however, there is a great deal of heterogeneity across countries and of in-country changes over time. On the former, the contrast between Haiti and Panama in growth performance is noteworthy. On the latter, the example of Chile is instructive: although the country's growth was mostly explained by structural reforms by Loayza, Fajnzylber, and Calderón (2005), the most important factor in explaining its recent growth performance seems to be external conditions. This does not mean that Chile's structural reform process stagnated or reversed, but only that its contribution to growth became quantitatively less relevant than that of external conditions.[4]

Such heterogeneity can also be seen in the benchmarking exercise, which shows that structural and stabilization features have a distinct impact on each country. This finding suggests that different paths to sustained growth are available to different countries. An immediate corollary is that growth strategies should be guided by pragmatism—and country-specific conditions—rather than by "recipes."[5]

Combined with a more widespread adoption of structural reform initiatives across the region, the commodity boom also facilitated the emergence of new "growth stars" in LAC. There is now a larger set of faster-growing countries in LAC than at the time of Loayza, Fajnzylber, and Calderón (2005), because of external conditions and structural reforms. Chile is now joined by countries such as Colombia, the Dominican Republic, Panama, and Peru as fast-growing LAC economies.[6]

What do these results imply for the region going forward? The continuing importance of structural reform as a growth driver and the fact that external conditions are projected to be less favorable[7] going forward bring structural domestic issues back to the forefront of the policy debate in LAC. At the same time, particularly in light of the risk of policy reversals in some countries, it is critical to stress the continuing importance of a sound macro-fiscal framework as a prerequisite for sustained growth, although the empirical analysis placed less weight on stabilization policies as growth engines.

The results from the empirical analysis in this study are also consistent with other recent work on growth in LAC:

- First, as recent research by Caselli (2016; reported in chapter 1) shows, countries in LAC could have been much closer to the United States in per capita income, given their human and physical capital endowments, if they did not suffer from a sizable efficiency (or total factor productivity) gap. Closing the efficiency gap would require structural reforms that improve resource allocation within the economy as well as incentives for economic agents to innovate.

- Second, as the global environment becomes less supportive, countries in the region will need to rely increasingly on domestic drivers of growth. Domestic demand has been a key factor in post-crisis recovery in the majority of countries. But to sustain growth into the medium term, supply-side domestic constraints might become binding. Although some countries have room to increase capacity utilization, many others are operating close to or above their possibility frontier (Talvi and Munyo 2013).

- Third, the structural reform agenda itself remains unfinished in LAC, as pointed out by Birdsall, Caicedo, and de la Torre (2010), thus indicating that plenty of scope exists for additional—and often unconventional—growth-enhancing structural reforms.[8]

All these distinct pieces of evidence point to the need for a renewed effort on the domestic structural front by countries in LAC. But the evidence also highlights the need for additional work that provides more granularity in specific policy interventions. The cross-country regressions undertaken for this report reemphasize the continuing importance of structural reforms for explaining past growth performance and evaluating future growth prospects. In so doing, the analysis helps to demystify claims that recent growth in LAC can be reduced to a mere response to favorable external conditions. However, the analysis says little about the specific interventions that could accelerate and sustain growth in individual countries. Therefore, it should be complemented by country-specific diagnostics and less disaggregated approaches that can shed light on the particular ways in which market imperfections and government failures interact with growth.[9]

Notes

1. It is useful to recall that macroeconomic policies that contribute to an unstable (volatile) economic environment increase uncertainty about future returns on investment. In doing so, such policies discourage physical capital accumulation and worsen longer-term growth prospects. For a discussion of these links, see Montiel (2011).

2. For example, as seen in chapter 3, the model predicts a considerably higher growth rate for Guyana and República Bolivariana de Venezuela than what was actually observed. Such predictions are mostly driven by external conditions. The difference between model predictions

and actual outcomes might indicate that poor macroeconomic policies and weak institutions impeded these countries from fully exploiting favorable external conditions.

3. These empirical results should not be interpreted as dismissing the importance of good governance for development. Governance variables might influence growth through other channels, as discussed in chapter 5.

4. This is all the more interesting because Loayza, Fajnzylber, and Calderón (2005, 4) concluded their study by postulating that, given its past performance in implementing structural reforms, "(…) Chile continues to have the best outlook for growth in the region."

5. For comparison, see de la Torre (2014).

6. De Gregorio (2014, 7) aptly summarizes this phenomenon: "Chile, the earliest reformer, enjoyed its highest growth during the 1990s. In other countries, most of the macroeconomic reforms occurred during the 1990s—including granting independence to central banks, consolidating fiscal policy, taking the first steps toward exchange rate flexibility, and other structural reforms—and these countries enjoyed the benefits almost a decade later."

7. Or, as argued by Talvi and Munyo (2013), external conditions have ceased to improve.

8. Birdsall, Caicedo, and de la Torre (2010, 27) highlight four main areas left out by the "Washington Consensus"-type approach, which would require active policy interventions: (i) volatility, (ii) institutions, (iii) knowledge and technological innovation, and (iv) equity.

9. The companion report, "What Is Preventing LAC from Converging to Higher Income Levels?", provides an attempt to generate more granularity by examining trends and structural bottlenecks at the sector and firm levels.

References

Birdsall, N., F. Caicedo, and A. de la Torre. 2010. "The Washington Consensus: Assessing a Damaged Brand." Policy Research Working Paper 5316, World Bank, Washington, DC.

Caselli, F., G. Esquivel, and F. Lefort. 1996. "Reopening the Convergence Debate: A New Look at Cross-Country Growth Empirics." *Journal of Economic Growth* 1: 363–90.

Caselli, Francesco. 2016. "The Latin American Efficiency Gap." In *Understanding Latin America and the Caribbean's Income Gap*, edited by J. Araujo, M. Clavijo, E. Vostroknutova, and K. Wacker. Washington, DC: World Bank.

De Gregorio, J. 2014. *How Latin America Weathered the Global Financial Crisis*. Washington, DC: Peterson Institute for International Economics.

de la Torre, A. 2014. "El Pensamiento sobre el Desarrollo Económico: De las Recetas al Pragmatismo." Presentation delivered at the Sixth Bolivian Conference on Economic Development. Cochabamba, Bolivia, August 28.

Loayza, Norman, Pablo Fajnzylber, and César Calderón. 2005. *Economic Growth in Latin America and the Caribbean: Stylized Facts, Explanations, and Forecasts*. Washington, DC: World Bank Group.

Montiel, P. 2011. *Macroeconomics in Emerging Markets*. Second edition. Cambridge, UK: Cambridge University Press.

Talvi, E., and I. Munyo. 2013. "Latin America Macroeconomic Outlook: A Global Perspective. Are the Golden Years for Latin America Over?" Brookings-CERES Macroeconomic Report. Brookings Institution, Washington, DC.

Appendix A: Setup and Estimation Methodology

The estimation strategy draws on advanced panel data techniques to estimate growth effects. It identifies these effects by exploring variation within countries over time, which avoids most basic biases caused by unobserved cross-country heterogeneity. A common approach in the empirical growth literature (see Durlauf, Johnson, and Temple 2005) has been to relate the change in the log of real gross domestic product (GDP) per capita between two periods to the lagged level of GDP per capita and a set of growth determinants. Following this literature, the baseline equation for a five-year non-overlapping panel for 1970–2010 is

$$\ln y_{ct} - \ln y_{ct-1} = \varphi \ln y_{ct-1} + \Gamma \ln(X)_{ct} + a_c + b_t + e_{ct} \tag{A.1}$$

where $\ln y_{ct} - \ln y_{ct-1}$ is the change in the natural log of real purchasing power parity (PPP) GDP per capita in country c between period t and period $t-1$; $\ln y_{ct-1}$ is the natural log of real PPP GDP per capita of country c in period $t-1$; a_c and b_t are country and year fixed effects, respectively; and e_{ct} is an error term.

The explanatory variables include proxies for structural and stabilization policies, as well as for transmission channels of the external shocks. As in Loayza, Fajnzylber, and Calderón (2005), the vector of growth determinants, X_{ct}, includes the logs of secondary school enrollment, the GDP share of domestic credit to the private sector, trade openness, government size, telephone lines per capita, inflation, the real exchange rate, an indicator of systemic banking crises, and the growth rate of the terms of trade. Additional variables that are included in X_{ct} are the Polity2 score, which is a measure of the degree of political competition and political constraints, as well as the growth rate of an international commodity export price index that captures windfalls from international commodity price booms.

The model includes country fixed effects to control for omitted fixed country characteristics, and time fixed effects to control for common external factors. The country fixed effects, a_c, capture cross-country differences in time-invariant factors such as fixed geographic characteristics (for example, distance to the equator, mountainous terrain, whether countries are landlocked, and natural resource endowments) as well as historical factors (for example, colonial origin, historical population density, exposure to the slave trade, and so forth) that may directly affect GDP per capita growth beyond their effect on X.

Early empirical work in the late 1980s and 1990s employed cross-section regressions to identify determinants of economic growth (see, for example, Mankiw, Romer, and Weil 1992). Although an advantage of cross-section regressions is that they have the potential to identify long-run relationships, this work has been criticized for being subject to severe endogeneity bias arising from omitted fixed country characteristics (see, for example, Durlauf, Johnson, and Temple 2005). The inclusion of country fixed effects in equation A.1 is therefore important to allay concerns that the estimates are biased because of the omission of historical and geographic variables. The year fixed effects capture (nonlinear) time trends and period-specific shocks that are common across countries. For example, they control for changes in the world technology frontier or global demand shocks that arise from changes in the world business cycle. Lagged GDP per capita is included in equation A.1 to control for conditional convergence.

Convergence in income per capita in this empirical model means convergence to each country's own steady state, but all results are identical to the model with convergence to a common steady state, the United States, because of the inclusion of time fixed effects. Lagged GDP per capita is included as an explanatory variable to control for convergence. In a cross-section regression, the hypothesis of (conditional) convergence is about whether poor countries grow faster than rich countries (conditional on country characteristics). In a panel regression that includes country fixed effects, the hypothesis of (conditional) convergence is about whether countries' GDP per capita growth is lower the closer they are to their country-specific steady state, a_c.[1] To see this, note that the country fixed effects capture among other factors cross-country differences in average GDP per capita, that is, whether countries are rich or poor. By including country fixed effects in the model, the estimated coefficients are identified by the within-country variation of the data. This, in turn, implies that the estimated convergence coefficient φ in the panel fixed effects model is *not* driven by poor countries growing faster than rich countries, and that the model therefore does not provide a framework to test for this concept of convergence. However, from a policy perspective, it is important to note that the determinants of growth identified in this framework are identical to the macroeconomic determinants of convergence. This becomes obvious looking at a model taking relative income to a common frontier, the United States, as the dependent variable. The estimation results about growth/convergence determinants are then identical, which is because of the inclusion of time fixed effects (see table B.8 in appendix B).

The shocks to the explanatory variables in this model have a long-run impact on the level of GDP per capita, but only a transitory effect on the growth rate. Steady-state convergence in the level of GDP per capita requires that $|\varphi| < 1$. Equation A.1 is estimated as follows:

$$\ln y_{ct} = \theta \ln y_{ct-1} + \Gamma \ln(X)_{ct} + a_c + b_t + e_{ct} \tag{A.1'}$$

where $\theta = 1 + \varphi$. This formulation makes it clear that, with $-1 < \theta < 1$, the estimated model is a stationary AR(1) model for the *level* of GDP per capita. In this model, a permanent perturbation to the level of X has a temporary (short-run) effect on GDP per capita growth. There is a permanent (long-run) effect on the level of GDP per capita but not on the GDP per capita growth rate.

This particular specification is an approximation around the steady state that allows testing for effects of common and country-specific responses to economic shocks. For interpretation, it is useful to note that the log-log specification of equation A.1 is not ad hoc, but rather follows from a first-order approximation around the steady state of any theoretical model that is nonlinear. Take, for example, the Solow-Swan growth model (see Romer 2011, chapter 1, for reference).[2] The simplest version of this neoclassical growth model allows the examination of the effects of capital accumulation via savings, s; long-run population growth, n; and long-run total factor productivity growth, g. A first-order approximation of growth around the steady state for each country, c, yields

$$\ln y_t - \ln y_{t-1} \approx \lambda[-\ln y_{t-1} + \alpha/(1-\alpha)\ln s_t - \alpha/(1-\alpha)\ln(g + n + \delta)] + \ln A_t \quad (A.2)$$

or, alternatively,

$$\ln y_t \approx (1-\lambda)\ln y_{t-1} + \lambda[\alpha/(1-\alpha)\ln s_t - \alpha/(1-\alpha)\ln(g + n + \delta)] + \ln A_t \quad (A.2')$$

where $\lambda = (n + g + \delta)*(\alpha/(1-\alpha))$ is the convergence rate between periods t and $t-1$; $\ln A_t$ is the level of total factor productivity in period t; δ is the depreciation rate of physical capital; and α is the capital-output elasticity. Equation A.2 is thus an AR(1) model that allows the analysis to characterize the dynamic response of GDP per capita to economic shocks for a particular country c. If we add to the time-series dimension of equation A.2 a cross-country dimension, then this yields

$$\ln y_{ct} \approx (1-\lambda_c)\ln y_{ct-1} + \lambda_c[\alpha/(1-\alpha)\ln s_{ct} - \alpha/(1-\alpha)\ln(g_c + n_c + \delta_c)] + \ln A_{ct} \quad (A.3)$$

An important point to note from equation A.3 is that, even if g is common across countries, as assumed, for example, in Mankiw, Romer, and Weil (1992), λ_c is country-specific. The reason is that in the data both population growth and physical capital depreciation rates differ across countries.[3] The effects of variables X_{ct} that affect economic growth through domestic savings, s_{ct}, will thus also have a country-specific growth effect.

The specific model choice is driven by the research question. The applied econometrics literature has used several different models for estimating growth regressions. Providing an overview treatment, Hauk and Wacziarg (2009), for example, suggest the use of a between-effects estimator that identifies the relevant parameters solely using data variation between countries (and not over time). This approach is especially informative if one is interested in highly persistent long-run drivers of growth. Studies emphasizing the role of institutions, geography, or legal heritage have highlighted the potential relevance of such variables for explaining long-run growth (for example, Acemoglu, Johnson, and Robinson 2001, 2002; Easterly and Levine 2003; Gallup, Sachs, and Mellinger 1998). This highlights, however, that the choice of the econometric model cannot rely on an objective single criterion that is independent of the research question, but that the latter is a relevant factor for evaluating the pros and cons of different econometric specifications. For example, studies focusing on the research question of model uncertainty and nonlinearities have advanced nonparametric and model-averaging techniques (for example, Henderson, Papageorgiou, and Parmeter 2012; Sala-i-Martin, Doppelhofer, and Miller 2004). Others have used methods they considered most appropriate to address the question whether the sources of growth differ for Africa (for example, Block 2001; Masanjala and Papageorgiou 2008; Crespo-Cuaresma 2010).

For the purpose of this study, we are most interested in estimating the parameters for those variables that vary considerably over time, as this might allow us to explain the recent growth performance in the Latin America and the Caribbean (LAC) region. However, we are not interested in explicitly estimating those country-specific parameters that capture drivers of growth that do not vary (considerably) over time and hence do not seem to be good candidates for explaining the latest uptick in growth, such as geographic or institutional variables. This research question calls for an identification strategy that uses data variation over time while controlling for unobserved heterogeneity across countries. This is allowed for with our panel data general method of moments (GMM) estimator, which uses country-fixed effects.[4]

We test for inconsistency of coefficient estimates that can arise from cross-country parameter heterogeneity. Cross-country parameter heterogeneity implies that the country-specific effects, φ_c and Γ_c, are part of the error term, e_{ct}, in equation A.1. If these country-specific effects are correlated with the right-hand-side variables ($\ln y_{ct-1}$ and $\ln(X)_{ct}$), then estimation of equation A.1 will yield inconsistent estimates of the average convergence rate, φ, as well as inconsistent estimates of the average marginal effects, Γ.[5] To check for cross-country parameter heterogeneity, we estimate the following:

$$\ln y_{ct} - \ln y_{ct-1} = \varphi_c \ln y_{ct-1} + \Gamma_c \ln(X)_{ct} + a_c + b_t + e_{ct} \qquad (A.4)$$

which gives us C different φ's and Γ's (where C is the number of cross-country units). If the average estimated φ_c and Γ_c are not significantly different from the estimated φ and Γ in equation A.1, then there is no evidence that cross-country parameter heterogeneity yields inconsistent estimates of the average marginal effects.

Using a system–general method of moments (system-GMM) estimator alleviates dynamic panel data biases. It is well known that dynamic panel estimation in the presence of country fixed effects yields biased estimates (Nickell 1981; Wooldridge 2002). To avoid this bias, we use system-GMM estimation.[6,7,8] Blundell and Bond (1998) showed that this estimator provides more efficient estimates than other instrumental variable estimators that use internal instruments, such as, for example, the Arellano-Bond (1991) first-difference GMM estimator that had been designed in earlier work to alleviate biases arising in dynamic panel regressions with fixed effects.

Internal instruments help correct for potential endogeneity bias. A further issue in the estimation of equation A.1 is that some of the growth determinants, X_{ct}, may themselves be a function of GDP per capita growth. We address this type of endogeneity bias by treating the relevant variables as endogenous regressors in the system-GMM estimation. In particular, we instrument endogenous variables (in levels) with lags of their first differences. We limit the instrument set to one lag to ensure that the number of instruments does not grow too large in the system-GMM estimation.[9]

Specification tests are run to ensure that estimates are consistent and the identification assumptions hold. The wide (and often imprudent) use of GMM and system-GMM techniques has led to skepticism toward this method. This skepticism is reasonable to the extent that the technique requires several econometric assumptions that have to be thoroughly checked, which has not always been the case in the empirical literature. To make sure the conditions for system-GMM estimation to yield consistent estimates are satisfied, we basically rely on three types of specifications tests. The first specification test is the Sargan test of the overidentifying restrictions. This is a joint test on the null hypothesis that the whole set of instruments is valid. Rejection of this null hypothesis is a red light that the model is misspecified.[10] The second set of specification tests examines whether the error term in equation A.1' is serially correlated. The standard method is to conduct tests for first- and second-order serial correlation of the residual in the first-difference equation. A correctly specified model should yield significant first-order serial correlation in the first-difference equation (no significant first-order serial correlation would suggest that the level of GDP per capita follows a random walk). If there is significant second-order serial correlation, then this would invalidate the use of first-order lags as instruments and require using higher-order lags as instruments. Finally, we also check whether identification in the first stage is strong (see table B.9 in appendix B), so the common pitfall of weak identification in "black-box" GMM estimation is avoided (see Bazzi and Clemens 2013; Kraay 2015).[11]

To capture the overall within-country unconditional effects of changes in each explanatory variable, and to ensure robustness to missing observations, balanced panel regressions are run for each subset of variables. Because some countries have missing observations during 1970–2010 for each subset of variables in the vector X, it is not feasible to conduct the panel regressions on a balanced panel when the full set of variables X is included in the regression model. Nevertheless, it is feasible to report estimates for a balanced panel for a subset of variables in X. In addition to reporting unbalanced panel estimates from the model that includes the entire vector of growth determinants, X, we thus report balanced panel estimates from a more parsimonious model that includes in the regression only one of the variables in the vector X. In this parsimonious model, the obtained estimates on each variable x should be interpreted as capturing the within-country unconditional effects. For example, financial development could be a channel through which schooling affects GDP per capita growth (say, because education is needed for the functioning of courts, and well-functioning courts are necessary for the enforcement of financial contracts). If we include both schooling and financial development in the model, then the estimated coefficient on schooling captures the (residual) effect that schooling has on GDP per capita growth beyond its effect via financial development. Ultimately, from a policy point of view, one may not care so much about this conditional effect but rather about the overall within-country effect that schooling has on economic growth. This within-country effect can be obtained by estimating the parsimonious but balanced panel model with only lagged GDP per capita and schooling as right-hand-side regressors (in addition to country and year fixed effects).

Robustness Checks

Balanced Panel

As one robustness check, we discuss estimates from balanced panel regressions. The baseline estimates, reported in the previous section, were obtained from a multivariate regression model. This model was estimated using the largest possible sample given data availability for the variables used in the estimation. Because not all variables are available for all countries and years during 1970–2010, the panel in the baseline regression is unbalanced. A balanced panel for the same multivariate model would reduce the number of available countries to only 36. We therefore opted to present balanced panel estimates for one dependent variable at a time but to preserve a higher number of countries in each of these regressions. Column 1 in table B.4 in appendix B presents estimates from a model that includes the variables of interest one at a time, controlling for lagged GDP as well as country and year fixed effects. In column 2 in table B.4, we add to the model the international commodity export price index to control for commodity price windfalls. This estimation strategy has the key advantage that it allows for a much larger sample. Since the variables are included in the model one at a time, the estimated coefficients should be interpreted as capturing unconditional effects. In columns 3 and 4, we repeat the regressions using data on real GDP per capita from Penn World Table (PWT) 8.0 rather than PWT 7.1.[12]

10-Year Panels

To check robustness and further smooth out business cycle fluctuations, we look at 10-year panels. Our baseline estimates are based on five-year non-overlapping panel data. In this section, we discuss estimates based on 10-year non-overlapping panels, reported in table B.12 in appendix B. As our interest is in exploring longer-run growth determinants, as opposed to determinants of business cycles, we chose five-year non-overlapping panel data instead of annual data as our benchmark to smooth out business cycle fluctuations while not compromising too much on reductions in the number of time-series observations. The 10-year panel data have the advantage that they allow further smoothing out business cycle fluctuations and analyzing effects that may materialize at longer lags; however, the 10-year panel data also come at a cost of reducing the number of time-series observations.

The 10-year panel analysis yields similar results to our baseline five-year analysis. Variables related to structural reforms, such as schooling, financial development, trade openness, and infrastructure, have a significant positive effect on GDP per capita growth, while the size of government has a significant negative effect. Quantitatively, the elasticity coefficients are around 0.1 for schooling and financial development, 0.15 for trade openness and infrastructure, and around -0.25 for government size. Political institutions have no significant effect on GDP per capita growth. Regarding variables related to stabilization policies, the 10-year panel analysis shows that inflation, the real exchange rate, and banking crises have a significant negative effect on GDP per capita growth; the elasticity coefficients on these variables are -0.14, -0.03, and -0.11, respectively.

Benchmarking Methodology

The benchmarking exercise constructs a counterfactual "what if" scenario to gain insights on where a country should start in reform implementation. The benchmark exercise consists of measuring what would have been a country's GDP per capita had it performed as the top regional performer on a given variable. It is intended as a first approximation to sequencing and prioritizing of reforms, and as an entry point for more in-depth country analysis.

The first step of the benchmarking exercise is determining the top regional performer in each of the explanatory variables of the model. This is done by looking at the country distribution for each of the explanatory variables (schooling, financial development, infrastructure, and so forth) and then determining the log-level of the country that is at the top decile of the distribution in each of those variables.

The next step is to construct the counterfactual income per capita. This is done by multiplying the log-level value of the top decile performer by the relevant unconditional effects estimated coefficient. This results in a counterfactual income per capita level if a specific country (for example, Colombia) had the log-level value in a variable (such as infrastructure) of the top decile performer (such as Chile, which was the top decile performer in the LAC distribution for the log-level values of infrastructure). With this result, a counterfactual per capita income is constructed for each country for that explanatory variable. The following flowchart depicts the steps in constructing the counterfactual level of income per capita:

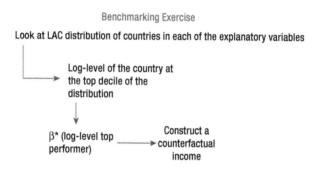

Benchmarking Exercise

Look at LAC distribution of countries in each of the explanatory variables

Log-level of the country at the top decile of the distribution

β^* (log-level top performer) ⟶ Construct a counterfactual income

The feasibility of the reforms entailed in the benchmarking exercise results would need to be determined by a country-specific assessment of implementation capacity and political economy issues, which is beyond the scope of this study. The goal of the exercise is to identify the structural and stabilization features that matter the most for each country vis-à-vis a chosen benchmark, rather than providing fully realistic simulations of policy changes. Although it is indeed unrealistic that countries will close those gaps that are largest, it seems reasonable to assume that any progress will most easily be made by policies concerning large existing gaps and the associated "low-hanging fruits," compared with gaps where countries are close to the frontier. Table B.3 in appendix B presents the country-specific standard deviations for each variable, which gives a sense of the realism of the assumed "jumps" for each country in the variables in the benchmarking exercise.

The benchmarking exercise that uses the unconditional effect estimated coefficients is consistent with our baseline GMM specification. The instrumentation in the unconditional estimation is adequate, since the estimate for the explanatory variable in the *second* stage allows the analysis to instrument for the level of the explanatory variable using various instruments in the *first* stage. Accordingly, in the baseline specification, the lagged explanatory variable is used in the instrument set for all the other explanatory variables in the unconditional effects regressions for efficiency reasons; that is, the purpose is to generate as much exogenous variation in the other explanatory variables in the first-stage regression as possible.

Notes

1. Convergence to a country's own steady state does not say anything about whether countries across the world will converge to the same level of GDP per capita.

2. In this model, the only way to generate long-run GDP per capita growth is through permanent total factor productivity (TFP) growth. A one-time increase in TFP will only have a long-run level effect (but lead to transitional GDP per capita growth). Similarly, a one-time increase in the domestic savings rate will only have a long-run level effect (but lead to transitional GDP per capita growth).

3. According to the World Bank's World Development Indicators (2013), the sample average of the annual population growth rate during 1970–2010 was around 3.2 percent, with a cross-country standard deviation of around 4.5 percent. Bu (2006) presents estimates of physical capital depreciation rates showing that these values are substantially higher for (poorer) countries located in the tropics.

4. An alternative option would be the use of co-integration methods that also focus on exploring the time dimension in panel data (Herzer 2008). However, this would pose much more stringent data requirements (such as annual availability for the data with at least 30 observations in the time dimension and assumptions about their stationarity properties) that are especially problematic for the lower-income countries in our sample and the LAC region.

5. For a formal discussion of parameter heterogeneity, see, for example, Pesaran and Shin (1995) or Philipps and Sul (2003).

6. To avoid overfitting the model, we use the "collapse" suboption in the STATA xtabond2 command. According to STATA, "the collapse suboption specifies that xtabond2 should create one instrument for each variable and lag distance, rather than one for each time period, variable, and lag distance. In large samples, collapse reduces statistical efficiency. But in small samples it can avoid the bias that arises as the number of instruments climbs toward the number of observations."

7. We use the one-step estimator to avoid severely downward biased standard errors associated with the two-step estimator (Blundell and Bond 1998).

8. Hauk and Wacziarg (2009) examine possible biases of GMM estimators in growth regressions using Monte Carlo simulations. Their finding is that GMM estimators can be severely biased in the presence of measurement error. The reason for this bias is a weak instrument problem, that is, classical measurement error attenuates the first-stage fit. Whether GMM estimators are biased because of measurement error therefore needs to be evaluated on a case-by-case basis by the strength of the first stage. We report estimates of the first-stage regressions underlying our system-GMM estimates in table B.9 in appendix B. These show a highly significant effect of lagged changes on levels and a highly significant effect of lagged levels on changes; hence, weak instrument bias is not an issue in our system-GMM regressions.

9. Limiting the instrument set in our framework is necessary, as system-GMM forces the empirical moments of instruments and residuals toward zero. At the same time, this condition is part of the overidentification statistic in the Sargan test. In the case of too many instruments, the system would have enough flexibility to make the exclusion restriction work by assumption, which is circumvented by limiting the instrument set (see Roodman 2009).

10. Rejection of this null hypothesis is necessary but not sufficient for the model to be well-specified. As Dollar and Kraay (2003) argue, it might be that a subset of instruments is weak, in which case one might fail to reject the null hypothesis of overall instrument validity ("type II error"). We therefore also report the significance of individual instruments in table B.9 in appendix B. Furthermore, showing the individual instrument significance is also instructive for the validity of instruments in the unconditional GMM regressions we use for the benchmarking exercise.

11. In this context, the individual t-statistics in table B.9 and furthermore the results of our unconditional model estimates are instructive, as they limit the weak-instrument problem in the case where various instruments appear strong in isolation but are highly correlated so that they are weak when used together (see Dollar and Kraay 2003).

12. Our main regressions are based on using PPP GDP per capita data from PWT 7.1. This database provides the largest number of country-year observations. It covers the period up to 2010 and 189 countries. In contrast, the recently available PPP GDP per capita data from PWT 8.0 covers the period up to 2011 and 167 countries.

References

Acemoglu, D., S. Johnson, and J. Robinson. 2001. "The Colonial Origins of Comparative Development: An Empirical Investigation." *American Economic Review* 91: 1369–1401.

———. 2002. "Reversal of Fortune: Geography and Institutions in the Making of the Modern World Income Distribution." *Quarterly Journal of Economics* 117 (4): 1231–94.

Arellano, M., and S. R. Bond. 1991. "Some Tests of Specification for Panel Data: Monte Carlo Evidence and an Application to Employment Equations." *Review of Economic Studies* 58 (2): 277–97.

Bazzi, Samuel, and Michael A. Clemens. 2013. "Blunt Instruments: Avoiding Common Pitfalls in Identifying the Causes of Economic Growth." *American Economic Journal: Macroeconomics* 5 (2): 152–86.

Block, S. A. 2001. "Does Africa Grow Differently?" *Journal of Development Economics* 65: 443–67.

Blundell, R., and S. Bond. 1998. "Initial Conditions and Moment Restrictions in Dynamic Panel Data Models." *Journal of Econometrics* 87: 115–43.

Bu, Y. 2006. "Fixed Capital Stock Depreciation in Developing Countries: Some Evidence from Firm Level Data." *Journal of Development Studies* 42: 881–901.

Easterly, W., and R. Levine. 2003. "Tropics, Germs and Crops: How Endowments Influence Economic Development." *Journal of Monetary Economics* 50 (1): 3–39.

Dollar, David, and Aart Kraay. 2003. "Institutions, Trade, and Growth." *Journal of Monetary Economics* 50 (1): 133–62.

Durlauf, S., P. Johnson, and J. Temple. 2005. "Growth Econometrics." In *Handbook of Economic Growth*, edited by P. Aghion and S. N. Durlauf. Amsterdam, Netherlands: North-Holland.

Crespo-Cuaresma, J. 2010. "How Different Is Africa? A Comment on Masanjala and Papageorgiou." *Journal of Applied Economics* 26 (6): 1041–47.

Gallup J. L., J. D. Sachs, and A. D. Mellinger. 1998. "Geography and Economic Development." NBER Working Paper 6849, National Bureau of Economic Research, Cambridge, MA.

Hauk, W., and R. Wacziarg. 2009. "A Monte Carlo Study of Growth Regressions." *Journal of Economic Growth* 14: 103–47.

Henderson, Daniel J., Chris Papageorgiou, and Christopher F. Parmeter. 2012. "Growth Empirics without Parameters." *Economic Journal* 122 (559): 125–54.

Herzer, Dierk. 2008. "The Long-Run Relationship between Outward FDI and Domestic Output: Evidence from Panel Data." *Economics Letters* 100: 146–49.

Kraay, Aart. 2015. 'Weak Internal Instruments in Dynamic Panel Growth Regressions: A Comment on "Redistribution, Inequality, and Growth." Policy Research Working Paper 7494, World Bank, Washington, DC.

Loayza, Norman, Pablo Fajnzylber, and César Calderón. 2005. *Economic Growth in Latin America and the Caribbean: Stylized Facts, Explanations, and Forecasts*. Washington, DC: World Bank Group.

Mankiw, G., D. Romer, and D. Weil. 1992. "A Contribution to the Empirics of Economic Growth." *Quarterly Journal of Economics* 107: 407–37.

Masanjala, W. H., and C. Papageorgiou. 2008. "Rough and Lonely Road to Prosperity: A Reexamination of the Sources of Growth in Africa Using Bayesian Model Averaging." *Journal of Applied Econometrics* 23 (5): 671–82.

Nickell, S. 1981. "Biases in Dynamic Models with Fixed Effects." *Econometrica* 49: 1417–26.

Phillips, P., and D. Sul. 2003. "Dynamic Panel Estimation and Homogeneity Testing under Cross Section Dependence." *Econometrics Journal* 6 (1): 217–59.

Romer, David. 2011. *Advanced Macroeconomics*. 4th edition. New York: McGraw-Hill.

Roodman, David. 2009. "A Note on the Theme of Too Many Instruments." *Oxford Bulletin of Economics and Statistics* 71 (1): 135–58.

Sala-i-Martin, Xavier, Gernot Doppelhofer, and Ronald I. Miller. 2004. "Determinants of Long-Term Growth: A Bayesian Averaging of Classical Estimates (BACE) Approach." *American Economic Review* 94 (4): 813–35.

Wooldridge, J. 2002. *Econometric Analysis of Cross Section and Panel Data.* Cambridge, MA: MIT Press.

World Bank. 2013. *World Development Indicators.* Online database. World Bank, Washington, DC. http://data.worldbank.org/indicator.

Appendix B: Tables and Figures

Description of Variables

Variable	Description	Source
Growth rate of GDP per capita	Change in the natural logarithm of real PPP GDP per capita between periods t and $t-1$	PWT 7.1
Lagged GDP per capita	Natural logarithm of real PPP GDP per capita in period $t-1$	PWT 7.1
Secondary schooling	Natural logarithm of secondary school enrollment rate	World Bank (2013)
Total years of schooling	Natural logarithm of total years of schooling in the population ages 25 and over	Barro and Lee (2010)
Credit/GDP	Natural logarithm of the ratio of domestic credit to the private sector divided by GDP. Domestic credit to private sector refers to financial resources provided to the private sector, such as through loans, purchases of nonequity securities, and trade credits and other accounts receivable, that establish a claim for repayment.	World Bank (2013)
Trade openness	Natural logarithm of the ratio of exports plus imports over PPP GDP adjusted for countries' population size	PWT 7.1
Telephone lines	Natural logarithm of main telephone lines per capita. Telephone lines are fixed telephone lines that connect a subscriber's terminal equipment to the public switched telephone network and that have a port on a telephone exchange. Integrated services digital network channels and fixed wireless subscribers are included.	World Bank (2013)
Mobile phones	Natural logarithm of mobile cellular telephone subscriptions are subscriptions to a public mobile telephone service using cellular technology, which provide access to the public switched telephone network. Post-paid and prepaid subscriptions are included.	World Bank (2013)
Government size	Logarithm of the ratio of government consumption expenditures over GDP	PWT 7.1
Polity2	The Polity2 score measures the degree of political constraints, political competition, and executive recruitment. It ranges between -10 and 10, with higher values denoting more democratic institutions.	Polity IV
CPI inflation	Natural logarithm of $100 +$ consumer price inflation rate. CPI inflation reflects the annual percentage change in the cost to the average consumer of acquiring a basket of goods and services.	World Bank (2013)
Real exchange rate	Natural logarithm of the GDP price level divided by the nominal exchange rate	PWT 7.1

(continued on next page)

Variable	Description	Source
Banking crisis	Indicator variable that is unity in period t if the country experienced a banking crisis	Reinhart and Rogoff (2011)
Terms of trade growth	Change in the natural logarithm of the net barter terms of trade index. The net barter terms of trade index is calculated as the percentage ratio of the export unit value indexes to the import unit value indexes, measured relative to the base year 2000.	World Bank (2013)
ComPI growth	Change in an international commodity export price index. The index is constructed as $$ComPI_{ct} = \prod_{i \in I} ComPrice_{it}^{\theta_{ic}}$$ where $ComPrice_{it}$ is the international price of commodity i in year t, and θ_{ic} is the average (time-invariant) value of exports of commodity i in the GDP of country c. Data on international commodity prices are from UNCTAD Commodity Statistics and data on the value of commodity exports are from the NBER-United Nations Trade Database (Feenstra et al. 2009). The commodities included in the index are aluminum, beef, cocoa, coffee, copper, cotton, gold, iron, maize, oil, rice, rubber, sugar, tea, tobacco, wheat, and wood.	Arezki and Brueckner (2012)

Note: ComPI = international commodity export price index; CPI = consumer price index; GDP = gross domestic product; PPP = purchasing power parity; PWT = Penn World Table.

TABLE B.2: List of Countries and Variable Frequencies

Country	GDP p.c. growth	Lagged GDP p.c.	Schooling	Credit/GDP	Openness	Telephones lines p.c.	Polity2	Government size	CPI inflation	Real exchange rate	Banking crisis	Terms of trade growth	ComPI growth
Afghanistan	8	8	7	4	8	8	5	8	2	8	8	2	8
Albania	8	8	7	4	8	8	8	8	6	8	8	2	8
Algeria	9	9	8	9	9	9	9	9	9	9	9	6	9
Angola	8	8	8	4	8	8	8	8	5	8	8	5	8
Antigua and Barbuda	8	8	5	7	8	8	0	8	7	8	8	2	0
Argentina	9	9	9	9	9	9	9	9	9	9	9	6	9
Armenia	3	3	3	3	3	3	3	3	3	3	3	2	3
Australia	9	9	5	9	9	9	9	9	9	9	9	2	9
Austria	9	9	8	9	9	9	9	9	9	9	9	2	9
Azerbaijan	3	3	3	3	3	3	3	3	3	3	3	2	3
Bahamas, The	8	8	8	8	8	8	0	8	8	8	8	2	8
Bahrain	8	8	8	7	8	8	8	8	5	8	8	2	8
Bangladesh	9	9	7	8	9	9	8	9	9	9	9	6	9
Barbados	9	9	7	9	9	9	0	9	9	9	9	2	9
Belarus	3	3	3	3	3	3	3	3	3	3	3	2	3
Belgium	9	9	8	9	9	9	9	9	9	9	9	2	0
Belize	8	8	6	7	8	8	0	8	8	8	8	2	8
Benin	9	9	6	9	9	9	9	9	9	9	9	6	9
Bermuda	8	8	4	0	8	8	0	8	8	8	8	2	8

(continued on next page)

93

TABLE B.2: **List of Countries and Variable Frequencies** *(continued)*

Country	GDP p.c. growth	Lagged GDP p.c.	Schooling	Credit/GDP	Openness	Telephones lines p.c.	Polity2	Government size	CPI inflation	Real exchange rate	Banking crisis	Terms of trade growth	ComPI growth
Bhutan	8	8	6	6	8	8	8	8	6	8	8	2	0
Bolivia	9	9	5	9	9	7	9	9	9	9	9	6	9
Bosnia and Herzegovina	4	4	1	3	4	4	1	4	4	4	4	2	4
Botswana	9	9	9	8	9	9	9	9	9	9	9	6	0
Brazil	9	9	6	9	9	9	9	9	9	9	9	6	9
Brunei Darussalam	8	8	8	3	8	7	0	8	5	8	8	2	0
Bulgaria	8	8	8	4	8	7	8	8	6	8	8	2	8
Burkina Faso	9	9	8	9	9	9	9	9	9	9	9	6	9
Burundi	9	9	7	7	9	9	9	9	9	9	9	6	9
Cabo Verde	9	9	7	7	9	8	0	9	6	9	9	6	0
Cambodia	8	8	5	4	8	5	7	8	4	8	8	2	8
Cameroon	9	9	8	9	9	8	9	9	9	9	9	6	9
Canada	9	9	8	9	9	9	9	9	9	9	9	2	9
Central African Republic	9	9	7	9	9	7	9	9	9	9	9	6	9
Chad	9	9	8	9	9	9	9	9	9	9	9	6	9
Chile	9	9	9	9	9	9	9	9	9	9	9	6	9
China Version	9	9	9	7	9	8	9	9	8	9	9	6	9
China Version	9	9	0	0	9	0	0	9	0	9	9	0	0

(continued on next page)

TABLE B.2: List of Countries and Variable Frequencies *(continued)*

Country	GDP p.c. growth	Lagged GDP p.c.	Schooling	Credit/GDP	Openness	Telephones lines p.c.	Polity2	Government size	CPI inflation	Real exchange rate	Banking crisis	Terms of trade growth	CompI growth
Colombia	9	9	9	9	9	9	9	9	9	9	9	6	9
Comoros	9	9	6	6	9	9	8	9	6	9	9	6	0
Congo, Dem. Rep.	9	9	8	9	9	9	9	9	9	9	9	6	9
Congo, Rep.	9	9	7	9	9	9	9	9	8	9	9	6	9
Costa Rica	9	9	9	9	9	9	9	9	9	9	9	6	9
Côte d'Ivoire	9	9	6	9	9	9	9	9	8	9	9	6	9
Croatia	4	4	4	4	4	4	4	4	4	4	4	2	4
Cuba	8	8	8	0	8	7	4	8	8	8	8	2	8
Cyprus	9	9	4	8	9	9	9	9	7	9	9	2	9
Czech Republic	4	4	4	4	4	4	4	4	4	4	4	2	4
Denmark	9	9	8	9	9	9	9	9	9	9	9	2	9
Djibouti	8	8	8	6	8	8	7	8	4	8	8	2	8
Dominica	8	8	8	7	8	8	0	8	7	8	8	2	0
Dominican Republic	9	9	8	9	9	7	9	9	9	9	9	6	9
Ecuador	9	9	8	9	9	9	9	9	6	9	9	6	9
Egypt, Arab Rep.	9	9	8	9	9	9	9	9	9	9	9	6	9
El Salvador	9	9	9	9	9	9	9	9	9	9	9	6	9

(continued on next page)

TABLE B.2: **List of Countries and Variable Frequencies** (*continued*)

Country	GDP p.c. growth	Lagged GDP p.c.	Schooling	Credit/GDP	Openness	Telephones lines p.c.	Polity2	Government size	CPI inflation	Real exchange rate	Banking crisis	Terms of trade growth	ComPI growth
Equatorial Guinea	9	9	6	6	9	6	9	9	4	9	9	5	9
Eritrea	3	3	3	3	3	3	3	3	3	3	3	3	0
Estonia	4	4	4	4	4	4	4	4	3	4	4	2	4
Ethiopia	9	9	7	6	9	9	9	9	6	9	9	3	9
Fiji	9	9	9	9	9	9	9	9	9	9	9	4	9
Finland	9	9	8	9	9	9	9	9	9	9	9	2	9
France	9	9	8	9	9	9	9	9	9	9	9	2	9
Gabon	9	9	7	9	9	6	9	9	9	9	9	6	9
Gambia, The	9	9	7	9	9	9	9	9	9	9	9	6	9
Georgia	3	3	3	3	3	3	3	3	3	3	3	2	3
Germany	8	8	0	0	8	0	5	8	0	8	8	0	8
Ghana	9	9	8	9	9	9	9	9	9	9	9	6	9
Greece	9	9	8	9	9	9	9	9	9	9	9	2	9
Grenada	8	8	7	7	8	8	0	8	7	8	8	2	0
Guatemala	9	9	9	9	9	9	9	9	9	9	9	6	9
Guinea	9	9	8	4	9	8	9	9	5	9	9	4	9
Guinea-Bissau	9	9	7	5	9	6	8	9	8	9	9	6	9
Guyana	8	8	7	8	8	8	8	8	8	8	8	2	8
Haiti	9	9	3	4	9	6	9	9	4	9	9	6	9
Honduras	9	9	7	9	9	8	9	9	9	9	9	6	9

(continued on next page)

TABLE B.2: **List of Countries and Variable Frequencies** (*continued*)

Country	GDP p.c. growth	Lagged GDP p.c.	Schooling	Credit/GDP	Openness	Telephones lines p.c.	Polity2	Government size	CPI inflation	Real exchange rate	Banking crisis	Terms of trade growth	ComPI growth
Hong Kong SAR, China	9	9	7	5	9	9	0	9	8	9	9	6	9
Hungary	8	8	8	6	8	8	8	8	8	8	8	2	8
Iceland	9	9	8	9	9	9	0	9	9	9	9	2	9
India	9	9	8	9	9	9	9	9	9	9	9	6	9
Indonesia	9	9	9	7	9	9	9	9	9	9	9	5	9
Iran, Islamic Rep.	9	9	8	9	9	9	9	9	9	9	9	2	9
Iraq	8	8	8	4	8	7	7	8	3	8	8	2	8
Ireland	9	9	8	9	9	9	9	9	2	9	9	2	9
Israel	9	9	8	9	9	9	9	9	9	9	9	2	9
Italy	9	9	8	9	9	9	9	9	9	9	9	2	9
Jamaica	9	9	8	9	9	9	9	9	9	9	9	2	9
Japan	9	9	8	9	9	9	9	9	7	9	9	2	9
Jordan	9	9	8	9	9	8	9	9	7	9	9	6	9
Kazakhstan	3	3	3	3	3	3	3	3	3	3	3	2	3
Kenya	9	9	8	9	9	9	9	9	9	9	9	6	9
Kiribati	8	8	8	0	8	7	0	8	8	8	8	2	8
Korea, Republic of	9	9	8	9	9	9	9	9	9	9	9	6	9
Kuwait	4	4	4	4	4	4	4	4	3	4	4	2	4

(*continued on next page*)

TABLE B.2: **List of Countries and Variable Frequencies** (*continued*)

Country	GDP p.c. growth	Lagged GDP p.c.	Schooling	Credit/GDP	Openness	Telephones lines p.c.	Polity2	Government size	CPI inflation	Real exchange rate	Banking crisis	Terms of trade growth	ComPI growth
Kyrgyz Republic	3	3	3	3	3	3	3	3	3	3	3	2	0
Lao PDR	8	8	8	5	8	8	8	8	6	8	8	2	8
Latvia	3	3	3	3	3	3	3	3	3	3	3	2	3
Lebanon	8	8	6	5	8	6	6	8	5	8	8	2	8
Lesotho	9	9	9	8	9	9	9	9	9	9	9	6	0
Liberia	8	8	3	8	8	6	8	8	8	8	8	4	8
Libya	4	4	2	4	4	4	4	4	3	4	4	2	4
Lithuania	3	3	3	3	3	3	3	3	3	3	3	2	3
Luxembourg	9	9	8	7	9	9	0	9	9	9	9	2	0
Macao SAR, China	8	8	7	6	8	6	0	8	6	8	8	2	0
Macedonia, FYR	4	4	4	4	4	4	4	4	4	4	4	2	0
Madagascar	9	9	6	9	9	8	9	9	9	9	9	6	9
Malawi	9	9	8	9	9	9	9	9	9	9	9	6	9
Malaysia	9	9	9	9	9	9	9	9	9	9	9	6	9
Maldives	8	8	6	7	8	7	0	8	3	8	8	2	0
Mali	9	9	8	9	9	9	9	9	8	9	9	6	9
Malta	8	8	8	8	8	8	0	8	8	8	8	2	8
Marshall Islands	8	8	3	0	8	6	0	8	6	8	8	2	0

(continued on next page)

TABLE B.2: **List of Countries and Variable Frequencies** (continued)

Country	GDP p.c. growth	Lagged GDP p.c.	Schooling	Credit/GDP	Openness	Telephones lines p.c.	Polity2	Government size	CPI inflation	Real exchange rate	Banking crisis	Terms of trade growth	ComPI growth
Mauritania	9	9	7	8	9	9	9	9	9	9	9	6	9
Mauritius	9	9	8	7	9	9	9	9	7	9	9	6	9
Mexico	9	9	8	9	9	9	9	9	9	9	9	6	9
Micronesia, Fed. Sts.	8	8	3	4	8	6	0	8	5	8	8	2	0
Moldova	3	3	3	3	3	3	3	3	3	3	3	2	0
Mongolia	8	8	8	4	8	6	8	8	6	8	8	2	8
Montenegro	4	4	2	2	4	2	1	4	2	4	4	0	0
Morocco	9	9	8	9	9	9	9	9	9	9	9	6	9
Mozambique	9	9	8	5	9	9	8	9	6	9	9	6	9
Namibia	9	9	5	5	9	9	5	9	6	9	9	6	0
Nepal	9	9	8	9	9	8	9	9	9	9	9	2	9
Netherlands	9	9	8	9	9	9	9	9	9	9	9	2	9
New Zealand	9	9	9	9	9	9	9	9	7	9	9	2	9
Nicaragua	9	9	9	9	9	9	9	9	9	9	9	6	9
Niger	9	9	8	9	9	9	9	9	8	9	9	6	9
Nigeria	9	9	8	9	9	6	9	9	9	9	9	6	9
Norway	9	9	8	9	9	9	9	9	9	9	9	2	9
Oman	8	8	8	8	8	8	8	8	6	8	8	2	8
Pakistan	9	9	7	9	9	9	9	9	9	9	9	6	9

(continued on next page)

TABLE B.2: **List of Countries and Variable Frequencies** *(continued)*

Country	GDP p.c. growth	Lagged GDP p.c.	Schooling	Credit/GDP	Openness	Telephones lines p.c.	Polity2	Government size	CPI inflation	Real exchange rate	Banking crisis	Terms of trade growth	ComPI growth
Palau	8	8	3	0	8	2	0	8	4	8	8	2	0
Panama	9	9	9	9	9	7	9	9	9	9	9	5	9
Papua New Guinea	9	9	7	8	9	9	8	9	9	9	9	2	9
Paraguay	9	9	9	9	9	9	9	9	9	9	9	6	9
Peru	9	9	9	9	9	9	9	9	9	9	9	6	9
Philippines	9	9	8	9	9	9	9	9	9	9	9	6	9
Poland	8	8	8	6	8	8	8	8	4	8	8	2	8
Portugal	9	9	7	9	9	9	9	9	9	9	9	2	9
Puerto Rico	9	9	1	0	9	8	0	9	9	9	9	0	0
Qatar	4	4	4	4	4	4	4	4	2	4	4	2	4
Romania	9	9	6	3	9	9	9	9	6	9	9	2	9
Russian Federation	4	4	4	4	4	4	4	4	4	4	4	2	4
Rwanda	9	9	8	8	9	9	9	9	9	9	9	6	9
Samoa	8	8	8	6	8	6	0	8	6	8	8	2	8
São Tomé and Príncipe	8	8	6	2	8	8	8	8	2	8	8	4	0
Saudi Arabia	4	4	2	4	4	4	0	4	4	4	4	2	4
Senegal	9	9	8	9	9	9	9	9	9	9	9	6	9

(continued on next page)

TABLE B.2: List of Countries and Variable Frequencies *(continued)*

Country	GDP p.c. growth	Lagged GDP p.c.	Schooling	Credit/GDP	Openness	Telephones lines p.c.	Polity2	Government size	CPI inflation	Real exchange rate	Banking crisis	Terms of trade growth	ComPI growth
Serbia	4	4	3	3	4	2	4	4	3	4	4	0	0
Seychelles	9	9	9	8	9	9	1	9	9	9	9	5	9
Sierra Leone	9	9	6	9	9	7	0	9	9	9	9	2	9
Singapore	9	9	0	9	9	9	9	9	9	9	9	6	9
Slovak Republic	4	4	4	4	4	4	4	4	4	4	4	2	4
Slovenia	4	4	4	4	4	4	4	4	4	4	4	2	4
Solomon Islands	8	8	8	7	8	6	4	8	4	8	8	4	0
Somalia	8	8	5	0	8	6	7	8	4	8	8	2	8
South Africa	9	9	5	9	9	9	9	9	9	9	9	6	9
Spain	9	9	8	9	9	9	9	9	9	9	9	2	9
Sri Lanka	9	9	7	9	9	9	9	9	9	9	9	6	9
St. Kitts and Nevis	8	8	6	7	8	6	8	8	7	8	8	2	0
St. Lucia	8	8	8	7	8	8	0	8	6	8	8	2	0
St. Vincent and the Grenadines	8	8	8	8	8	8	0	8	8	8	8	2	0
Sudan	8	8	8	8	8	8	0	8	8	8	8	6	8
Suriname	8	8	7	8	8	8	0	8	7	8	8	2	8

(continued on next page)

TABLE B.2: List of Countries and Variable Frequencies *(continued)*

Country	GDP p.c. growth	Lagged GDP p.c.	Schooling	Credit/GDP	Openness	Telephones lines p.c.	Polity2	Government size	CPI inflation	Real exchange rate	Banking crisis	Terms of trade growth	ComPI growth
Swaziland	8	8	7	8	8	8	0	8	8	8	8	6	0
Sweden	9	9	8	9	9	9	9	9	9	9	9	2	9
Switzerland	9	9	7	8	9	9	9	9	6	9	9	2	0
Syrian Arab Republic	9	9	8	9	9	9	9	9	9	9	9	2	0
Taiwan, China	9	9	0	0	9	0	0	9	0	9	9	0	0
Tajikistan	3	3	3	3	3	3	3	3	3	3	3	2	3
Tanzania	9	9	7	5	9	9	9	9	5	9	9	4	9
Thailand	9	9	8	9	9	9	9	9	9	9	9	6	9
Timor-Leste	2	2	0	0	2	0	0	2	0	2	2	0	0
Togo	9	9	8	9	9	8	9	9	9	9	9	6	9
Tonga	8	8	8	8	8	7	0	8	6	8	8	2	0
Trinidad and Tobago	9	9	8	9	9	9	0	9	9	9	9	4	9
Tunisia	9	9	8	9	9	9	9	9	9	9	9	6	9
Turkey	9	9	8	9	9	9	9	9	9	9	9	6	9
Turkmenistan	3	3	0	2	9	3	3	3	3	3	3	2	3
Uganda	9	9	9	9	9	9	9	9	6	9	9	5	9

(continued on next page)

TABLE B.2: List of Countries and Variable Frequencies *(continued)*

Country	GDP p.c. growth	Lagged GDP p.c.	Schooling	Credit/GDP	Openness	Telephones lines p.c.	Polity2	Government size	CPI inflation	Real exchange rate	Banking crisis	Terms of trade growth	ComPI growth
Ukraine	3	3	3	3	3	3	3	3	3	3	3	2	3
United Arab Emirates	4	4	4	4	4	4	0	4	4	4	4	2	4
United Kingdom	9	9	8	9	9	9	9	9	9	9	9	2	9
United States	9	9	8	9	9	9	9	9	9	9	9	6	9
Uruguay	9	9	9	9	9	9	9	9	9	9	9	6	9
Uzbekistan	4	4	4	0	4	4	4	4	4	4	4	2	4
Vanuatu	8	8	8	7	8	8	0	8	7	8	8	2	0
Venezuela, RB	9	9	8	9	9	9	9	9	9	9	9	6	9
Vietnam	8	8	5	4	8	6	7	8	5	8	8	2	8
Yemen, Rep.	4	4	3	4	4	4	4	4	4	4	4	2	4
Zambia	9	9	6	9	9	9	9	9	9	9	9	6	9
Zimbabwe	9	9	7	7	9	9	9	9	5	9	9	6	9

TABLE B.3: Country-Specific Standard Deviations

Country	GDP p.c. growth	ln GDP p.c.	ln schooling	ln credit/GDP	ln trade openness	ln gov. cons./GDP	ln telephone lines	Inflation	Real exchange rate
Argentina	0.0965178	0.2083769	0.2401638	0.2759639	0.3479453	0.2612056	0.6243829	2.2110820	0.3643913
Belize	0.0693043	0.3079661	0.1022013	0.3487259	0.1116230	0.1136226	0.8735070	0.7027453	0.2864807
Bolivia	0.0905950	0.0904809	0.5290284	1.2385780	0.1616475	0.3946878	0.4910722	1.9623780	0.6663238
Brazil	0.1281178	0.4871118	0.5515332	0.5547065	0.3087695	0.1120239	1.1552840	1.7959130	0.3238280
Chile	0.1042575	0.4357949	0.2410770	0.8753646	0.3075319	0.2498778	0.9773171	1.2780060	0.2287116
Colombia	0.0547157	0.3245587	0.4321094	0.1799386	0.2187969	0.3988311	0.8475138	0.5510521	0.2609790
Costa Rica	0.0875417	0.2957874	0.3631774	0.3869106	0.2394945	0.1773092	1.2281720	0.8144322	0.1615058
Cuba	0.1813303	0.2786204	0.4091353	–	0.2061999	0.0601340	0.5341700	1.0253450	0.2125148
Dominica	0.0629833	0.4526888	0.1931214	0.2538443	0.0816500	0.1371845	1.1325920	0.7364681	0.1200997
Dominican Republic	0.0934589	0.5188949	0.3692364	0.6277146	0.2745736	0.2729278	0.7439834	0.8099455	0.2410947
Ecuador	0.1066276	0.3342828	0.2436950	0.1612192	0.0905198	0.1898644	0.8732558	0.6533860	0.1947675
El Salvador	0.0982602	0.2090906	0.3780768	0.2836004	0.2019515	0.2188363	1.2430330	0.7360144	0.7257872
Grenada	0.1065796	0.6026588	0.3512709	0.3547951	0.1660342	0.1814549	1.2064690	0.4112015	0.1792495
Guatemala	0.0888754	0.2711643	0.5940946	0.3043539	0.2752157	0.1435356	1.0940110	0.9817654	0.1398485
Guyana	0.1540460	0.1843370	0.1241873	0.6368911	0.3217861	0.2222525	1.0416920	0.9996848	0.4146806
Honduras	0.0732468	0.1750156	0.5412481	0.5012690	0.2716118	0.1303834	1.0628660	0.5820990	0.1647486
Haiti	0.0846865	0.0818713	0.2095421	0.1582483	0.4399328	0.1257787	0.4345213	0.4835521	0.1964860
Jamaica	0.1242766	0.1982560	0.2210154	0.2406645	0.1380458	0.4033966	0.9679167	0.5495867	0.1508347

(continued on next page)

TABLE B.3: **Country-Specific Standard Deviations** *(continued)*

Country	GDP p.c. growth	In GDP p.c.	In schooling	In credit/GDP	In trade openness	In gov. cons./GDP	In telephone lines	Inflation	Real exchange rate
St. Kitts and Nevis	0.0911674	0.6252608	0.1259977	0.2070505	0.1479346	0.0836326	0.7879448	0.3328319	0.1701756
St. Lucia	0.1225927	0.4486403	0.4551427	0.3109451	0.1307696	0.0695333	1.0107570	0.3508641	0.1334926
Mexico	0.0798520	0.3620831	0.3910040	0.2723466	0.4663839	0.2331915	1.0304160	0.9814607	0.1747584
Nicaragua	0.1542405	0.2412113	0.4746547	0.2929395	0.2180955	0.5438398	0.6842079	2.4615460	0.3503949
Panama	0.0981952	0.5301425	0.1940668	0.5097725	0.2596523	0.2204348	0.3444512	0.6664418	0.1806710
Peru	0.1235278	0.2090934	0.3084570	0.2354268	0.2621915	0.0980454	0.8671290	1.9489600	0.2450706
Paraguay	0.0985568	0.3206538	0.5321751	0.4087829	0.2977318	0.1099519	0.9449003	0.6672755	0.2272985
Uruguay	0.1234097	0.2570460	0.2122892	0.3757726	0.3899448	0.1553905	0.7118576	0.8600272	0.2812153
St.Vincent and the Grenadines	0.0798308	0.4655725	0.5439714	0.1734355	0.1503752	0.0695561	0.9568596	0.5524530	0.1508840
Venezuela, RB	0.1190661	0.1447098	0.2100130	0.5356786	0.2578176	0.1348014	0.8101301	0.998036	0.2628537

TABLE B.4: **Economic Growth Regressions**
(unconditional effects, five-year balanced panel)

	Dependent variable: ln(GDP p.c.)			
	(1)	(2)	(3)	(4)
	SYS GMM	SYS GMM	SYS GMM	SYS GMM
Variable	PWT 7.1 data	PWT 7.1 data	PWT 8.0 data	PWT 8.0 data
	Panel A: Schooling			
ln(secondary school enrollment rate), t	0.06** (0.03)	0.08*** (0.03)	0.06 (0.05)	0.10** (0.05)
ln(GDP p.c.), t−1	0.79*** (0.04)	0.80*** (0.04)	0.72** (0.04)	0.69*** (0.05)
ComPI growth, t		1.69** (0.69)		2.64*** (0.88)
AR (1) test, p-value	0.00	0.00	0.00	0.00
AR (2) test, p-value	0.13	0.31	0.15	0.37
Sargan test χ^2(2), p-value	0.33	0.58	0.76	0.12
Country FE	Yes	Yes	Yes	Yes
Year FE	Yes	Yes	Yes	Yes
Observations	760	664	680	608
Countries	95	83	85	76
	Panel B: Financial development			
ln(private domestic credit/GDP), t	0.10*** (0.03)	0.09*** (0.03)	0.05* (0.02)	0.06** (0.03)
ln(GDP p.c.), t−1	0.68*** (0.05)	0.69*** (0.05)	0.69*** (0.04)	0.67*** (0.05)
ComPI growth, t		1.11** (0.54)		2.67*** (0.75)
AR (1) test, p-value	0.00	0.00	0.00	0.00
AR (2) test, p-value	0.00	0.00	0.00	0.01
Sargan test χ^2(2), p-value	0.34	0.55	0.59	0.87
Country FE	Yes	Yes	Yes	Yes
Year FE	Yes	Yes	Yes	Yes
Observations	800	744	744	696
Countries	100	93	93	87

(continued on next page)

	Dependent variable: ln(GDP p.c.)			
	(1)	(2)	(3)	(4)
	SYS GMM	SYS GMM	SYS GMM	SYS GMM
Variable	PWT 7.1 data	PWT 7.1 data	PWT 8.0 data	PWT 8.0 data
	Panel C: Trade openness			
ln(structure adjusted trade volume/GDP), t	0.11*** (0.03)	0.11*** (0.03)	0.14*** (0.04)	0.14*** (0.04)
ln(GDP p.c.), $t-1$	0.82*** (0.03)	0.81*** (0.03)	0.74*** (0.04)	0.71*** (0.04)
ComPI growth, t		1.53*** (0.56)		2.75*** (0.74)
AR (1) test, p-value	0.00	0.00	0.00	0.00
AR (2) test, p-value	0.00	0.00	0.00	0.00
Sargan test χ^2(2), p-value	0.56	0.65	0.50	0.91
Country FE	Yes	Yes	Yes	Yes
Year FE	Yes	Yes	Yes	Yes
Observations	1,272	1,032	1,096	920
Countries	159	129	137	115
	Panel D: Government size			
ln(government consumption/GDP), t	−0.09* (0.05)	−0.07 (0.05)	−0.32*** (0.07)	−0.25*** (0.08)
ln(GDP p.c.), $t-1$	0.82*** (0.03)	0.81*** (0.03)	0.76*** (0.03)	0.73*** (0.03)
ComPI growth, t		1.76*** (0.55)		2.81*** (0.74)
AR (1) test, p-value	0.00	0.00	0.00	0.00
AR (2) test, p-value	0.00	0.00	0.00	0.00
Sargan test χ^2(2), p-value	0.41	0.13	0.98	0.63
Country FE	Yes	Yes	Yes	Yes
Year FE	Yes	Yes	Yes	Yes
Observations	1,272	1,032	1,096	920
Countries	159	129	137	115

(continued on next page)

TABLE B.4: **Economic Growth Regressions** *(continued)*

Variable	Dependent variable: ln(GDP p.c.)			
	(1)	(2)	(3)	(4)
	SYS GMM	SYS GMM	SYS GMM	SYS GMM
	PWT 7.1 data	PWT 7.1 data	PWT 8.0 data	PWT 8.0 data
	Panel E: Infrastructure			
ln(telephone lines p.c.), t	0.08***	0.08***	0.04**	0.05**
	(0.01)	(0.01)	(0.02)	(0.02)
ln(GDP p.c.), $t-1$	0.75***	0.73***	0.75***	0.73***
	(0.03)	(0.03)	(0.03)	(0.03)
ComPI growth, t		0.83*		1.42**
		(0.49)		(0.67)
AR (1) test, p-value	0.00	0.00	0.00	0.00
AR (2) test, p-value	0.00	0.00	0.00	0.00
Sargan test χ^2(2), p-value	0.22	0.26	0.49	0.20
Country FE	Yes	Yes	Yes	Yes
Year FE	Yes	Yes	Yes	Yes
Observations	976	824	896	760
Countries	122	103	112	95
	Panel F: Political institutions			
ln(Polity2 score), t	0.003	0.002	0.006	0.006
	(0.003)	(0.003)	(0.004)	(0.004)
ln(GDP p.c.), $t-1$	0.78***	0.75***	0.73***	0.71***
	(0.04)	(0.04)	(0.03)	(0.03)
ComPI growth, t		2.10***		3.36***
		(0.61)		(0.86)
AR (1) test, p-value	0.00	0.00	0.00	0.00
AR (2) test, p-value	0.00	0.00	0.00	0.00
Sargan test χ^2(2), p-value	0.74	0.81	0.32	0.58
Country FE	Yes	Yes	Yes	Yes
Year FE	Yes	Yes	Yes	Yes
Observations	920	848	864	792
Countries	115	106	108	99

(continued on next page)

Variable	(1) SYS GMM PWT 7.1 data	(2) SYS GMM PWT 7.1 data	(3) SYS GMM PWT 8.0 data	(4) SYS GMM PWT 8.0 data
Dependent variable: ln(GDP p.c.)				
Panel G: Lack of price stability				
Inflation rate, t	−0.07** (0.03)	−0.05* (0.03)	−0.09** (0.04)	−0.08** (0.04)
ln(GDP p.c.), t−1	0.77*** (0.03)	0.78*** (0.03)	0.70*** (0.04)	0.70*** (0.04)
ComPI growth, t		2.16*** (0.71)		4.85*** (0.95)
AR (1) test, p-value	0.00	0.00	0.00	0.00
AR (2) test, p-value	0.00	0.00	0.01	0.08
Sargan test χ^2(2), p-value	0.71	0.80	0.52	0.62
Country FE	Yes	Yes	Yes	Yes
Year FE	Yes	Yes	Yes	Yes
Observations	784	720	712	656
Countries	98	90	89	82
Panel H: Real exchange rate				
ln(real exchange rate), t	−0.08** (0.03)	−0.07** (0.03)	−0.11* (0.06)	−0.10 (0.06)
ln(GDP p.c.), t−1	0.79*** (0.03)	0.79*** (0.03)	0.74*** (0.03)	0.72*** (0.04)
ComPI growth, t		1.39** (0.57)		3.82*** (0.82)
AR (1) test, p-value	0.00	0.00	0.00	0.00
AR (2) test, p-value	0.00	0.00	0.00	0.01
Sargan test χ^2(2), p-value	0.17	0.11	0.17	0.07
Country FE	Yes	Yes	Yes	Yes
Year FE	Yes	Yes	Yes	Yes
Observations	784	720	712	656
Countries	98	90	89	82

(continued on next page)

TABLE B.4: **Economic Growth Regressions** *(continued)*

Variable	Dependent variable: ln(GDP p.c.)			
	(1)	(2)	(3)	(4)
	SYS GMM	SYS GMM	SYS GMM	SYS GMM
	PWT 7.1 data	PWT 7.1 data	PWT 8.0 data	PWT 8.0 data
	Panel I: Banking crises			
Banking crisis, t	−0.08***	−0.07***	−0.06**	−0.06**
	(0.02)	(0.02)	(0.03)	(0.03)
ln(GDP p.c.), $t-1$	0.83***	0.81***	0.76***	0.74***
	(0.03)	(0.03)	(0.03)	(0.03)
ComPI growth, t		1.92***		3.34***
		(0.55)		(0.73)
AR (1) test, p-value	0.00	0.00	0.00	0.00
AR (2) test, p-value	0.00	0.00	0.00	0.00
Sargan test $\chi^2(2)$, p-value	0.12	0.09	0.15	0.25
Country FE	Yes	Yes	Yes	Yes
Year FE	Yes	Yes	Yes	Yes
Observations	1,272	1,032	1,096	920
Countries	159	129	137	115

Note: The dependent variable is real GDP per capita. The method of estimation is system-GMM (system–general method of moments). For each panel and column, the system-GMM estimation is based on two endogenous variables and four instruments. ComPI = international commodity export price index; FE = fixed effects; GDP = gross domestic product; p.c. = per capita; PWT = Penn World Table; SYS GMM = system–general method of moments; t = time.
*Significantly different from zero at the 10 percent significance level, ** 5 percent significance level, *** 1 percent significance level.

TABLE B.5: **Economic Growth Regressions**
(alternative measures of schooling)

	Dependent variable: ln(GDP p.c.)		
	(1)	(2)	(3)
Variable	SYS GMM	SYS GMM	SYS GMM
ln(primary school enrollment rate), t	0.07 (0.06)		
ln(tertiary school enrollment rate), t		0.05*** (0.02)	
Average years of schooling, t			0.19* (0.10)
ln(GDP p.c.), $t-1$	0.80*** (0.04)	0.75*** (0.04)	0.82*** (0.05)
AR (1) test, p-value	0.00	0.00	0.00
AR (2) test, p-value	0.08	0.00	0.25
Sargan test $\chi^2(2)$, p-value	0.16	0.21	0.61
Country FE	Yes	Yes	Yes
Year FE	Yes	Yes	Yes
Observations	757	660	632
Countries	95	92	79

Note: The dependent variable is real GDP per capita. The method of estimation is system-GMM (system–general method of moments). The system-GMM estimations are based on two endogenous variables and four instruments. FE = fixed effects; GDP = gross domestic product; p.c. = per capita; SYS GMM = system–general method of moments; t = time.
*Significantly different from zero at the 10 percent significance level, ** 5 percent significance level, *** 1 percent significance level.

TABLE B.6: Economic Growth Regressions
(alternative measures of infrastructure)

Variable	Dependent variable: ln(GDP p.c.)		
	(1)	(2)	(3)
	SYS GMM	SYS GMM	SYS GMM
ln(GDP p.c.), $t-1$	0.65***	0.53***	0.66***
	(0.04)	(0.10)	(0.04)
ln(mobile phones), t	0.02***		
	(0.00)		
ln(roads), t		0.31**	
		(0.15)	
ln(railways), t			0.24***
			(0.08)
AR (1) test, p-value	0.00	0.00	0.19
AR (2) test, p-value	0.48	0.68	0.09
Sargan test $\chi^2(2)$, p-value	0.44	0.27	0.41
Country FE	Yes	Yes	Yes
Year FE	Yes	Yes	Yes
Observations	526	626	573
Countries	122	181	110

Note: The dependent variable is real GDP per capita. The method of estimation is system-GMM (system–general method of moments). The system-GMM estimations are based on two endogenous variables and four instruments. FE = fixed effects; GDP = gross domestic product; p.c. = per capita; SYS GMM = system–general method of moments; t = time.
*Significantly different from zero at the 10 percent significance level, ** 5 percent significance level, *** 1 percent significance level.

Economic Growth Regressions
(Are the effects in Latin American countries significantly different?)

	Dependent variable: ln(GDP p.c.)			
Variable	(1)	(2)	(3)	(4)
	Panel A: Schooling			
ln(secondary school enrollment rate), t	0.06** (0.03)	0.05* (0.03)	0.07** (0.03)	0.08*** (0.03)
LAC*ln(secondary school enrollment rate), t	−0.01 (0.01)	−0.01 (0.01)	−0.02 (0.01)	−0.02 (0.01)
ln(GDP p.c.), $t-1$	0.78*** (0.04)	0.80*** (0.04)	0.82*** (0.04)	0.82*** (0.04)
LAC*ln(GDP p.c.), $t-1$		0.00 (0.09)	−0.16 (0.11)	−0.15 (0.12)
ComPI growth, t			1.78** (0.68)	1.75** (0.69)
LAC*ComPI growth, t				1.33 (3.24)
AR (1) test, p-value	0.00	0.00	0.00	0.00
AR (2) test, p-value	0.14	0.14	0.37	0.37
Sargan test, p-value	0.46	0.15	0.58	0.58
Country FE	Yes	Yes	Yes	Yes
Year FE	Yes	Yes	Yes	Yes
Observations	760	760	664	664
Countries	95	95	83	83
	Panel B: Financial development			
ln(private domestic credit/GDP), t	0.07** (0.03)	0.08*** (0.03)	0.07** (0.03)	0.07** (0.03)
LAC*ln(private domestic credit/GDP), t	0.01 (0.03)	0.00 (0.01)	0.00 (0.01)	0.00 (0.01)
ln(GDP p.c.), $t-1$	0.70*** (0.05)	0.66*** (0.05)	0.68*** (0.05)	0.68*** (0.05)
LAC*ln(GDP p.c.), $t-1$		0.15** (0.07)	0.13* (0.07)	0.12 (0.07)
ComPI growth, t			0.93* (0.53)	0.83 (0.56)
LAC*ComPI growth, t				1.16 (1.52)
Country FE	Yes	Yes	Yes	Yes
Year FE	Yes	Yes	Yes	Yes

(continued on next page)

Variable	Dependent variable: ln(GDP p.c.)			
	(1)	(2)	(3)	(4)
AR (1) test, p-value	0.00	0.00	0.00	0.00
AR (2) test, p-value	0.00	0.00	0.00	0.00
Sargan test, p-value	0.10	0.29	0.33	0.27
Observations	800	800	744	744
Countries	100	100	93	93
Panel C: Trade openness				
ln(structure adjusted trade volume/GDP), t	0.14*** (0.03)	0.14*** (0.03)	0.13*** (0.03)	0.13*** (0.03)
LAC*ln(structure adjusted trade volume/GDP), t	−0.25** (0.11)	−0.22** (0.10)	−0.11 (0.09)	−0.11 (0.09)
ln(GDP p.c.), $t-1$	0.81*** (0.03)	0.80*** (0.03)	0.80*** (0.03)	0.80*** (0.03)
LAC*ln(GDP p.c.), $t-1$		0.05 (0.05)	−0.01 (0.07)	−0.02 (0.07)
ComPI growth, t			1.44** (0.56)	1.53*** (0.59)
LAC*ComPI growth, t				−1.00 (1.70)
AR (1) test, p-value	0.00	0.00	0.00	0.00
AR (2) test, p-value	0.00	0.00	0.00	0.00
Sargan test, p-value	0.24	0.21	0.15	0.16
Country FE	Yes	Yes	Yes	Yes
Year FE	Yes	Yes	Yes	Yes
Observations	1,272	1,272	1,032	1,032
Countries	159	159	129	129
Panel D: Government size				
ln(government consumption/ GDP), t	−0.09* (0.05)	−0.11** (0.06)	−0.11* (0.06)	−0.11** (0.06)
LAC*ln(government consumption/GDP), t	0.07 (0.06)	−0.00 (0.03)	−0.05 (0.05)	−0.05 (0.04)
ln(GDP p.c.), $t-1$	0.83*** (0.03)	0.82*** (0.03)	0.82*** (0.04)	0.82*** (0.04)
LAC*ln(GDP p.c.), $t-1$		0.02 (0.09)	−0.20 (0.19)	−0.20 (0.19)

(continued on next page)

	Dependent variable: ln(GDP p.c.)			
Variable	(1)	(2)	(3)	(4)
ComPI growth, t			1.85*** (0.57)	2.00** (0.60)
LAC*ComPI growth, t				−1.85 (1.79)
AR (1) test, p-value	0.00	0.00	0.00	0.00
AR (2) test, p-value	0.00	0.00	0.00	0.00
Sargan test, p-value	0.35	0.83	0.95	0.94
Country FE	Yes	Yes	Yes	Yes
Year FE	Yes	Yes	Yes	Yes
Observations	1,272	1,272	1,032	1,032
Countries	159	159	129	129
	Panel E: Infrastructure			
ln(telephone lines p.c.), t	0.08*** (0.01)	0.08*** (0.01)	0.08*** (0.01)	0.08*** (0.01)
LAC*ln(telephone lines p.c.), t	0.00 (0.01)	−0.01 (0.01)	−0.01 (0.01)	−0.01 (0.01)
ln(GDP p.c.), $t-1$	0.75*** (0.02)	0.80*** (0.02)	0.79*** (0.03)	0.79*** (0.03)
LAC*ln(GDP p.c.), $t-1$		−0.00 (0.04)	−0.08 (0.06)	−0.08 (0.06)
ComPI growth, t			0.98** (0.50)	0.99** (0.52)
LAC*ComPI growth, t				−0.06 (1.34)
AR (1) test, p-value	0.00	0.00	0.00	0.00
AR (2) test, p-value	0.00	0.00	0.00	0.00
Sargan test, p-value	0.38	0.29	0.42	0.41
Country FE	Yes	Yes	Yes	Yes
Year FE	Yes	Yes	Yes	Yes
Observations	976	976	824	824
Countries	122	122	103	103
	Panel F: Political institutions			
ln(Polity2 score), t	0.003 (0.004)	0.003 (0.004)	0.002 (0.004)	0.002 (0.004)

(continued on next page)

Variable	(1)	(2)	(3)	(4)
LAC*ln(Polity2 score), t	−0.003	−0.005	−0.005	−0.005
	(0.004)	(0.003)	(0.003)	(0.003)
ln(GDP p.c.), $t-1$	0.77***	0.78***	0.76***	0.76***
	(0.04)	(0.04)	(0.04)	(0.04)
LAC*ln(GDP p.c.), $t-1$		−0.02	−0.09	−0.10
		(0.08)	(0.09)	(0.10)
ComPI growth, t			2.28***	2.46***
			(0.60)	(0.63)
LAC*ComPI growth, t				−1.47
				(1.68)
AR (1) test, p-value	0.00	0.00	0.00	0.00
AR (2) test, p-value	0.00	0.00	0.00	0.00
Sargan test, p-value	0.66	0.52	0.55	0.40
Country FE	Yes	Yes	Yes	Yes
Year FE	Yes	Yes	Yes	Yes
Observations	920	920	864	792
Countries	115	115	108	99
Panel G: Lack of price stability				
Inflation rate, t	−0.07*	−0.06*	−0.05***	−0.05***
	(0.04)	(0.04)	(0.02)	(0.02)
LAC*inflation rate, t	0.00	0.01	0.02	0.02
	(0.01)	(0.02)	(0.01)	(0.01)
ln(GDP p.c.), $t-1$	0.77***	0.75***	0.74***	0.74***
	(0.03)	(0.04)	(0.03)	(0.03)
LAC*ln(GDP p.c.), $t-1$		0.13	0.13	0.13
		(0.08)	(0.03)	(0.08)
ComPI growth, t			1.87***	2.06***
		(0.61)		(0.65)
LAC*ComPI growth, t				−1.41
				(1.51)
AR (1) test, p-value	0.00	0.00	0.00	0.00
AR (2) test, p-value	0.00	0.00	0.00	0.00
Sargan test, p-value	0.83	0.84	0.22	0.22
Country FE	Yes	Yes	Yes	Yes
Year FE	Yes	Yes	Yes	Yes

(continued on next page)

Variable	Dependent variable: ln(GDP p.c.)			
	(1)	(2)	(3)	(4)
Observations	784	784	720	720
Countries	98	98	90	90
	Panel H: Real exchange rate			
ln(real exchange rate), t	−0.15**	−0.13***	−0.13***	−0.12***
	(0.06)	(0.04)	(0.04)	(0.04)
LAC*ln(real exchange rate), t	0.02	−0.02	−0.02	−0.02
	(0.09)	(0.01)	(0.01)	(0.01)
ln(GDP p.c.), $t-1$	0.79***	0.79***	0.80***	0.80***
	(0.04)	(0.04)	(0.04)	(0.04)
LAC*ln(GDP p.c.), $t-1$		−0.03	−0.08	−0.08
		(0.10)	(0.11)	(0.11)
ComPI growth, t			1.36**	1.49***
			(0.58)	(0.62)
LAC*ComPI growth, t				−0.93
				(1.47)
AR (1) test, p-value	0.00	0.00	0.00	0.00
AR (2) test, p-value	0.00	0.00	0.00	0.00
Sargan test, p-value	0.77	0.85	0.57	0.61
Country FE	Yes	Yes	Yes	Yes
Year FE	Yes	Yes	Yes	Yes
Observations	784	784	720	720
Countries	98	98	90	90
	Panel I: Banking crises			
Banking crisis, t	−0.08***	−0.08***	−0.05**	−0.05**
	(0.03)	(0.03)	(0.02)	(0.02)
LAC*banking crisis, t	0.01	0.01	−0.01	−0.02
	(0.07)	(0.07)	(0.05)	(0.05)
ln(GDP p.c.), $t-1$	0.83***	0.83***	0.67***	0.67***
	(0.03)	(0.03)	(0.04)	(0.04)
LAC*ln(GDP p.c.), $t-1$		0.00	−0.13	−0.14
		(0.05)	(0.09)	(0.09)
ComPI growth, t			1.68***	1.82***
			(0.53)	(0.54)
LAC*ComPI growth, t				−1.53
				(1.68)
AR (1) test, p-value	0.00	0.00	0.00	0.00

(continued on next page)

TABLE B.7: **Economic Growth Regressions** *(continued)*

Variable	Dependent variable: ln(GDP p.c.)			
	(1)	(2)	(3)	(4)
AR (2) test, p-value	0.00	0.00	0.00	0.01
Sargan test, p-value	0.06	0.10	0.11	0.11
Country FE	Yes	Yes	Yes	Yes
Year FE	Yes	Yes	Yes	Yes
Observations	1,272	1,272	1,032	1,032
Countries	159	159	129	129

Note: The dependent variable is real GDP per capita. The method of estimation is system-GMM (system–general method of moments). ComPI = international commodity export price index; FE = fixed effects; GDP = gross domestic product; LAC = Latin America and the Caribbean; p.c. = per capita; t = time.
*Significantly different from zero at the 10 percent significance level, ** 5 percent significance level, *** 1 percent significance level.

FIGURE B.1: **Kernel Density Plot and Histogram of Country-Specific Coefficients for Policy Variables of Interest**

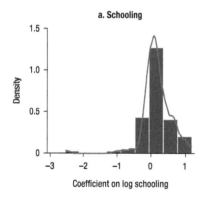
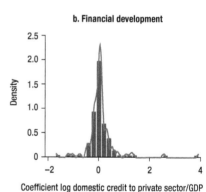

a. Schooling

b. Financial development

(continued on next page)

FIGURE B.1: **Kernel Density Plot and Histogram of Country-Specific Coefficients for Policy Variables of Interest** *(continued)*

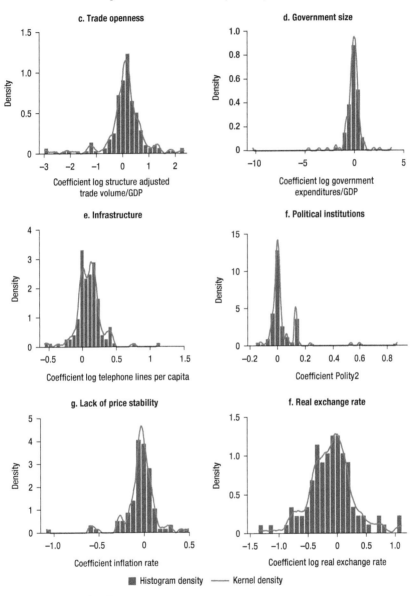

Note: GDP = gross domestic product.

TABLE B.8: **Economic Growth Regressions**
(Time heterogeneity: Post 1990s)

	Dependent variable: ln(GDP p.c.)	
	(1)	(2)
	SYS GMM	SYS GMM
Variable	Linear term	Post-1990 interaction
ln(GDP p.c.), $t-1$	0.85***	−0.03***
	(0.03)	(0.01)
ln(secondary school enrollment rate), t	0.06**	−0.00
	(0.03)	(0.02)
ln(private domestic credit/GDP), t	0.10***	−0.01
	(0.03)	(0.02)
ln(structure adjusted trade volume/GDP), t	0.19***	−0.15
	(0.07)	(0.10)
ln(government consumption/GDP), t	−0.10**	0.02
	(0.05)	(0.02)
ln(telephone lines p.c.), t	0.12***	0.03***
	(0.02)	(0.01)
Polity2 score, t	−0.002	−0.001
	(0.002)	(0.002)
Inflation rate, t	−0.04**	0.01
	(0.02)	(0.14)
ln(real exchange rate), t	−0.16***	0.02
	(0.05)	(0.05)
Banking crisis, t	−0.07***	−0.04
	(0.02)	(0.05)

(continued on next page)

TABLE B.8: **Economic Growth Regressions** *(continued)*

	Dependent variable: ln(GDP p.c.)	
	(1)	(2)
	SYS GMM	SYS GMM
Variable	Linear term	Post-2000 interaction
ln(GDP p.c.), $t-1$	0.80***	−0.03***
	(0.03)	(0.01)
ln(secondary school enrollment rate), t	0.05	−0.03
	(0.03)	(0.03)
ln(private domestic credit/GDP), t	0.12***	−0.04
	(0.03)	(0.03)
ln(structure adjusted trade volume/GDP), t	0.18***	−0.10
	(0.06)	(0.08)
ln(government consumption/GDP), t	−0.10**	0.02
	(0.05)	(0.03)
ln(telephone lines p.c.), t	0.11***	0.02
	(0.03)	(0.01)
Polity2 score, t	−0.002	−0.003
	(0.002)	(0.002)
Inflation rate, t	−0.04	−0.02
	(0.07)	(0.19)
ln(real exchange rate), t	−0.14***	−0.03
	(0.04)	(0.03)
Banking crisis, t	−0.07***	−0.04
	(0.02)	(0.06)

Note: The dependent variable is real GDP per capita. The method of estimation is system-GMM (system–general method of moments). GDP = gross domestic product; p.c. = per capita; SYS GMM = system–general method of moments; t = time. *Significantly different from zero at the 10 percent significance level, ** 5 percent significance level, *** 1 percent significance level.

TABLE B.9: **Economic Growth Regressions**
(GDP per capita relative to the United States)

Dependent variable: ln(GDP p.c. relative to the United States)

Variable	(1) SYS GMM	(2) LS
ln(GDP p.c.), $t-1$	0.78*** (0.06)	0.75*** (0.03)
Structural policies and institutions		
ln(secondary school enrollment rate), t	0.02 (0.05)	−0.03 (0.03)
ln(private domestic credit/GDP), t	0.07*** (0.03)	0.02 (0.02)
ln(structure adjusted trade volume/GDP), t	0.08* (0.05)	0.10*** (0.03)
ln(government consumption/GDP), t	−0.26*** (0.04)	−0.13*** (0.03)
ln(telephone lines p.c.), t	0.14*** (0.03)	0.08*** (0.02)
Polity2 score, t	−0.00 (0.03)	−0.01 (0.02)
Stabilization policies		
Inflation rate, t	−0.01 (0.01)	−0.01* (0.01)
ln(real exchange rate), t	−0.06 (0.04)	−0.02 (0.03)
Banking crisis, t	−0.04 (0.03)	−0.05* (0.03)
External conditions		
ComPI growth, t	10.48*** (2.69)	6.96*** (2.59)
Terms-of-trade growth, t	0.12*** (0.03)	0.11*** (0.03)
AR (1) test, p-value	0.02	–
AR (2) test, p-value	0.10	–
Sargan test $\chi^2(10)$, p-value	0.13	–
Country FE	Yes	Yes
Year FE	Yes	Yes
Observations	464	464
Countries	126	126

Note: The dependent variable is real GDP per capita. The method of estimation in column (1) is system-GMM (system–general method of moments); column (2) least squares. The system-GMM estimation is based on 10 endogenous variables and 20 instruments. En dashes indicate that these tests were not performed for the least-squares regressions. ComPI = international commodity export price index; FE = fixed effects; GDP = gross domestic product; LS = least squares; p.c. = per capita; SYS GMM = system–general method of moments; t = time.
*Significantly different from zero at the 10 percent significance level, ** 5 percent significance level, *** 1 percent significance level.

TABLE B.10: **First-Stage Regressions for System-GMM**

Dependent variable:	ln(GDP p.c.)	ln(secondary school enrollment rate)	ln(private domestic credit/GDP)	ln(structure adjusted trade volume/GDP)	ln(government consumption/GDP)	ln(telephone lines p.c.)	Polity2 score	Inflation rate	ln(real exchange rate)	Banking crisis
	(1)	(2)	(3)	(4)	(5)	(6)	(7)	(8)	(9)	(10)
					Panel A: Level equation					
Lagged first difference	0.73***	0.18***	0.54***	0.59***	0.55***	0.78***	0.48***	0.25***	0.33***	0.12***
	(0.05)	(0.05)	(0.04)	(0.04)	(0.03)	(0.05)	(0.04)	(0.03)	(0.04)	(0.03)
					Panel B: First-difference equation					
Lagged level	−0.012***	−0.131***	−0.043***	−0.163***	−0.066***	−0.027***	−0.115***	−0.375***	−0.145***	−0.75***
	(0.003)	(0.008)	(0.013)	(0.018)	(0.008)	(0.005)	(0.014)	(0.027)	(0.017)	(0.04)

Note: We report the significance level of each single variable, as a joint test (as the Sargan test for overidentifying restrictions reported in the regression tables, for example) might hide the possibility that a subset of instruments is weak, which might cause problems for inference (see Dollar and Kraay 2003). GDP = gross domestic product; GMM = general method of moments; p.c. = per capita.

*Significantly different from zero at the 10 percent significance level, ** 5 percent significance level, *** 1 percent significance level.

TABLE B.11: **Economic Growth Regressions**
(interaction effects for Caribbean countries; estimates of linear terms not reported)

Variable	Dependent variable: ln(GDP p.c.)								
	(1)	(2)	(3)	(4)	(5)	(6)	(7)	(8)	(9)
	SYS GMM	SYS GMM	SYS GMM	SYS GMM	SYS GMM	SYS GMM	SYS GMM	SYS GMM	SYS GMM
ln(secondary school enrollment rate), t*Caribbean dummy	0.13* (0.07)								
ln(private domestic credit/GDP, t*Caribbean dummy		−0.33 (0.51)							
ln(structure adjusted trade volume /GDP), t*Caribbean dummy			0.34 (0.35)						
ln(government consumption/GDP, t*Caribbean dummy				0.13 (0.50)					
ln(telephone lines p.c.), t*Caribbean dummy					0.01 (0.02)				
Polity2 score, t*Caribbean dummy						0.00 (0.02)			
Inflation rate, t*Caribbean dummy							0.08 (0.17)		
ln(real exchange rate), t*Caribbean dummy								−0.75 (2.99)	
Banking crisis, t*Caribbean dummy									0.09 (0.80)

(continued on next page)

124

TABLE B.11: **Economic Growth Regressions** *(continued)*

Variable	(1) SYS GMM	(2) SYS GMM	(3) SYS GMM	(4) SYS GMM	(5) SYS GMM	(6) SYS GMM	(7) SYS GMM	(8) SYS GMM	(9) SYS GMM
					Dependent variable: ln(GDP p.c.)				
AR (1) test, p-value	0.00	0.00	0.00	0.00	0.00	0.00	0.00	0.00	0.00
AR (2) test, p-value	0.16	0.00	0.00	0.00	0.00	0.00	0.00	0.00	0.00
Sargan test, p-value	0.35	0.47	0.39	0.25	0.37	0.54	0.82	0.77	0.06
Country FE	Yes	Yes	Yes	Yes	Yes	Yes	Yes	Yes	Yes
Year FE	Yes	Yes	Yes	Yes	Yes	Yes	Yes	Yes	Yes
Observations	760	800	1,272	1,272	976	920	784	784	1,272
Countries	95	100	159	159	122	115	98	98	159

Note: The dependent variable is real GDP per capita. The method of estimation is system-GMM (system–general method of moments). FE = fixed effects; GDP = gross domestic product; p.c. = per capita; SYS GMM = system–general method of moments; *t* = time.

*Significantly different from zero at the 10 percent significance level, ** 5 percent significance level, *** 1 percent significance level.

TABLE B.12: Economic Growth Regressions
(country-specific coefficients)

Country	Coefficient	Standard error	Country	Coefficient	Standard error	Country	Coefficient	Standard error
				Panel A: Schooling				
Algeria	−0.012	0.108	Guatemala	−0.011	0.093	Niger	−0.089	0.091
Angola	0.787	0.152	Guinea	−0.087	0.116	Norway	0.561	0.469
Argentina	0.265	0.277	Hungary	0.530	0.611	Oman	0.042	0.037
Austria	0.638	1.029	Iceland	−0.151	0.348	Panama	1.080	0.526
Bahamas, The	−2.544	1.079	India	0.515	0.175	Paraguay	−0.062	0.098
Bahrain	−0.483	0.267	Indonesia	0.150	0.119	Peru	0.255	0.211
Belgium	0.180	0.215	Iran, Islamic Rep.	0.273	0.154	Philippines	0.183	0.437
Botswana	0.022	0.060	Iraq	−0.013	0.274	Poland	0.852	0.393
Brunei Darussalam	−0.656	0.246	Ireland	0.681	0.416	Rwanda	0.032	0.075
Bulgaria	−0.943	2.911	Israel	0.263	0.473	Samoa	−0.237	0.535
Burkina Faso	0.018	0.052	Italy	−0.054	0.278	Senegal	0.012	0.131
Cameroon	−0.202	0.151	Jamaica	−0.133	0.212	Seychelles	0.058	0.123
Canada	0.529	0.804	Japan	−0.146	1.060	Solomon Islands	−0.047	0.139
Chad	0.156	0.070	Jordan	1.060	0.484	Spain	0.068	0.259
Chile	0.873	0.361	Kiribati	−0.081	0.084	St. Lucia	0.142	0.099
China	0.459	0.157	Korea, Republic of	0.536	0.298	St. Vincent and the Grenadines	0.263	0.089

(continued on next page)

Country	Coefficient	Standard error	Country	Coefficient	Standard error	Country	Coefficient	Standard error
Colombia	0.081	0.120	Lao PDR	0.424	0.116	Sudan	0.282	0.113
Congo, Dem. Rep.	0.206	0.217	Lesotho	0.058	0.120	Sweden	0.247	0.207
Costa Rica	0.134	0.137	Luxembourg	0.481	0.267	Syrian Arab Republic	−0.208	0.278
Cuba	0.865	0.262	Malawi	−0.093	0.134	Thailand	0.073	0.098
Denmark	0.403	0.427	Malaysia	0.263	0.304	Togo	−0.124	0.125
Djibouti	0.049	0.109	Mali	0.035	0.067	Tonga	1.185	0.666
Dominica	0.206	0.259	Malta	−0.098	0.453	Trinidad and Tobago	−0.129	0.292
Dominican Republic	0.203	0.177	Mauritius	0.279	0.142	Tunisia	0.008	0.082
Ecuador	−0.089	0.286	Mexico	−0.074	0.160	Turkey	0.158	0.100
Egypt, Arab Rep.	0.603	0.166	Mongolia	0.819	0.401	Uganda	0.143	0.083
El Salvador	0.120	0.153	Morocco	0.095	0.136	United Kingdom	0.615	0.517
Fiji	−0.211	0.554	Mozambique	0.171	0.081	United States	0.557	1.039
Finland	0.596	0.558	Nepal	0.169	0.132	Uruguay	0.293	0.249
France	0.060	0.330	Netherlands	0.298	0.302	Vanuatu	−0.016	0.071
Ghana	0.675	0.345	New Zealand	0.292	0.256	Venezuela, RB	0.074	0.258
Greece	0.235	0.554	Nicaragua	0.048	0.153	Mean (Median)	0.168 (0.143)	

(continued on next page)

TABLE B.12: **Economic Growth Regressions** *(continued)*

Country	Coefficient	Standard error	Country	Coefficient	Standard error	Country	Coefficient	Standard error
				Panel B: Financial development				
Algeria	0.025	0.102	Gambia, The	0.066	0.133	Pakistan	1.249	3.751
Argentina	−1.036	0.810	Ghana	0.086	0.131	Panama	0.036	0.388
Australia	0.112	0.149	Greece	0.010	0.169	Papua New Guinea	0.346	0.773
Austria	0.203	0.711	Guatemala	−0.215	0.404	Paraguay	−0.367	0.589
Bahamas, The	−0.232	0.442	Guyana	−0.445	0.364	Peru	3.938	13.891
Bangladesh	0.088	0.174	Honduras	0.140	1.534	Philippines	−0.099	0.469
Barbados	0.023	0.209	Iceland	−0.036	0.098	Portugal	−0.031	0.192
Belgium	0.053	0.287	India	0.316	0.337	Senegal	0.067	0.301
Benin	0.086	0.164	Iran, Islamic Rep.	−0.137	0.684	Seychelles	−0.140	0.204
Bolivia	−0.073	0.243	Ireland	0.193	0.146	Sierra Leone	0.331	0.172
Botswana	−0.199	0.721	Israel	−0.145	0.561	Singapore	−0.184	0.795
Brazil	−0.015	0.271	Italy	−0.155	0.312	South Africa	−0.114	0.295
Burkina Faso	−0.161	0.879	Jamaica	2.555	3.883	Spain	−0.019	0.197
Burundi	−0.463	0.222	Japan	0.390	0.586	Sri Lanka	0.062	1.125
Cameroon	0.157	0.162	Jordan	1.085	0.645	St. Vincent and the Grenadines	0.098	0.894
Canada	0.031	0.330	Kenya	0.582	1.079	Sudan	0.096	0.104

(continued on next page)

TABLE B.12: **Economic Growth Regressions** *(continued)*

Country	Coefficient	Standard error	Country	Coefficient	Standard error	Country	Coefficient	Standard error
Central African Republic	−0.071	0.283	Korea, Republic of	0.489	0.278	Suriname	0.122	0.218
Chad	0.010	0.183	Lesotho	−0.145	0.317	Swaziland	0.324	0.592
Chile	−0.233	0.223	Liberia	−0.031	0.418	Sweden	−0.100	0.970
Colombia	0.479	1.162	Madagascar	0.333	0.319	Syrian Arab Republic	−0.469	1.222
Congo, Dem. Rep.	0.073	0.132	Malawi	0.320	0.418	Thailand	0.076	0.457
Congo, Republic of	0.132	0.122	Malaysia	−0.112	0.364	Togo	0.241	0.639
Costa Rica	0.070	0.162	Mali	−0.047	0.455	Tonga	0.701	0.346
Côte d'Ivoire	0.183	0.179	Malta	0.146	0.225	Trinidad and Tobago	−1.197	0.473
Cyprus	0.037	0.158	Mexico	0.006	0.467	Tunisia	−0.753	1.580
Denmark	−0.027	0.113	Morocco	−0.008	0.276	Turkey	0.142	0.299
Dominican Republic	−0.140	0.886	Nepal	0.146	0.215	Uganda	0.234	0.171
Ecuador	−1.695	5.414	Netherlands	−0.023	0.273	United Kingdom	0.073	0.175
Egypt, Arab Rep.	0.311	0.276	New Zealand	0.031	0.154	United States	0.107	0.267
El Salvador	−0.186	0.601	Nicaragua	1.356	0.829	Uruguay	−0.361	0.315
Fiji	−0.122	0.257	Niger	0.053	0.147	Venezuela, RB	0.029	0.119
Finland	−0.262	0.559	Nigeria	−0.300	0.320	Zambia	0.079	0.253
France	0.790	3.300	Norway	0.067	0.424	Mean (Median)	0.097 (0.045)	
Gabon	0.082	0.740	Oman	0.581	2.085			

(continued on next page)

TABLE B.12: **Economic Growth Regressions** *(continued)*

Country	Coefficient	Standard error	Country	Coefficient	Standard error	Country	Coefficient	Standard error
				Panel C: Trade openness				
Australia	0.290	0.223	Guatemala	−0.188	1.143	Panama	−0.056	1.108
Austria	0.152	0.207	Guinea	0.048	0.489	Papua New Guinea	0.170	0.601
Bahamas, The	−0.155	0.274	Guinea-Bissau	−0.398	0.210	Paraguay	−0.402	0.525
Bahrain	0.578	0.342	Guyana	0.181	0.237	Peru	0.540	0.563
Bangladesh	0.172	0.203	Haiti	−0.102	0.217	Philippines	−0.013	0.210
Barbados	−0.538	1.006	Honduras	0.286	0.303	Poland	0.176	0.089
Belgium	0.154	0.205	Hong Kong SAR, China	0.137	0.115	Portugal	0.104	0.171
Belize	−2.043	3.233	Hungary	0.024	0.074	Puerto Rico	2.351	2.892
Benin	−0.063	0.478	Iceland	−0.241	0.386	Romania	0.475	0.244
Bermuda	−1.128	2.632	India	0.378	0.122	Rwanda	−0.103	0.105
Bhutan	0.762	0.235	Indonesia	0.114	1.227	Samoa	−1.181	1.817
Bolivia	0.426	1.428	Iran, Islamic Rep.	0.158	0.193	São Tomé and Príncipe	−0.168	0.248
Botswana	−0.229	0.180	Iraq	0.296	0.203	Senegal	0	0.315
Brazil	−0.069	0.187	Ireland	0.348	0.107	Seychelles	−0.049	0.102
Brunei Darussalam	1.850	0.972	Israel	0.312	1.342	Sierra Leone	0.663	0.211
Bulgaria	0.733	0.384	Italy	0.024	0.180	Singapore	0.503	0.201

(continued on next page)

TABLE B.12: **Economic Growth Regressions** *(continued)*

Country	Coefficient	Standard error	Country	Coefficient	Standard error	Country	Coefficient	Standard error
Burkina Faso	−0.080	0.178	Jamaica	1.379	1.182	Solomon Islands	0.335	0.170
Burundi	1.102	0.366	Japan	0.051	0.229	Somalia	0.278	0.084
Cabo Verde	−3.004	0.972	Korea, Republic of	0.689	0.188	St. Kitts and Nevis	−0.044	0.457
Cambodia	0.228	0.056	Jordan	−0.200	0.233	South Africa	0.579	0.535
Cameroon	−1.351	2.120	Kenya	−0.214	0.408	Spain	0.103	0.104
Canada	0.124	0.259	Kiribati	−0.118	0.215	Sri Lanka	1.391	1.144
Central African Republic	0.366	0.351	Lao PDR	0.242	0.094	St. Lucia	−2.209	1.619
Chad	−1.231	1.068	Lebanon	−0.377	0.520	St. Vincent and the Grenadines	−0.694	0.422
Chile	0.733	0.255	Lesotho	−0.233	3.532	Sudan	0.141	0.160
China, Version 1	0.660	0.098	Liberia	1.028	0.162	Suriname	0.061	2.512
China, Version 2	0.328	0.059	Luxembourg	0.537	0.514	Swaziland	−0.211	0.303
Colombia	0.011	0.278	Macao SAR, China	−1.788	0.609	Sweden	0.096	0.154
Comoros	1.255	0.405	Madagascar	0.141	0.205	Switzerland	−0.023	0.235
Congo, Dem. Rep.	−0.147	0.300	Malawi	0.557	0.279	Syrian Arab Republic	−0.579	1.367
Congo, Republic of	0.522	0.737	Malaysia	0.451	0.250	Taiwan, China	0.906	0.276
Costa Rica	0.113	0.307	Maldives	−1.238	0.266	Tanzania	0.153	0.279
Côte d'Ivoire	0.581	0.404	Mali	−0.959	1.560	Thailand	0.239	0.177
Cuba	−0.038	0.536	Malta	0.781	0.708	Togo	−0.699	0.448

(continued on next page)

131

TABLE B.12: Economic Growth Regressions *(continued)*

Country	Coefficient	Standard error	Country	Coefficient	Standard error	Country	Coefficient	Standard error
Cyprus	2.200	2.255	Marshall Islands	1.258	0.686	Tonga	−0.190	0.331
Denmark	0.139	0.171	Mauritania	−2.626	2.929	Trinidad and Tobago	0.329	0.358
Djibouti	0.108	0.294	Mauritius	0.032	1.420	Tunisia	0.936	1.421
Dominica	0.390	0.767	Mexico	−0.035	0.090	Turkey	0.161	0.129
Dominican Republic	0.546	1.192	Micronesia, Fed. Sts.	−0.204	0.475	Uganda	−0.484	0.604
Ecuador	0.209	1.018	Mongolia	0.424	0.417	United Kingdom	0.254	0.227
Egypt, Arab Rep.	−0.352	0.169	Morocco	0.464	0.532	United States	0.120	0.154
El Salvador	−0.033	0.284	Mozambique	0.636	0.521	Uruguay	0.181	0.144
Equatorial Guinea	1.814	0.143	Namibia	0.122	0.246	Vanuatu	0.310	0.382
Ethiopia	0.340	0.424	Nepal	0.190	0.512	Venezuela, RB	−0.166	1.026
Fiji	0.814	1.237	Netherlands	0.122	0.163	Vietnam	0.597	0.170
Finland	0.130	0.179	New Zealand	0.177	0.230	Zambia	0.290	0.185
France	0.025	0.179	Nicaragua	0.063	0.261	Zimbabwe	−0.541	0.212
						Mean (Median)	0.0866 (0.130)	
Panel D: Government burden								
Afghanistan	−0.490	0.197	Gabon	−0.785	0.535	Niger	0.198	0.209
Albania	0.429	0.366	Gambia, The	0.102	0.147	Nigeria	0.139	0.096
Algeria	−0.844	1.244	Germany	0.137	0.364	Norway	0.081	0.667
Angola	−0.490	0.161	Ghana	−0.387	0.943	Oman	−0.187	0.658

(continued on next page)

TABLE B.12: **Economic Growth Regressions** *(continued)*

Country	Coefficient	Standard error	Country	Coefficient	Standard error	Country	Coefficient	Standard error
Antigua and Barbuda	0.468	0.707	Greece	-0.157	1.014	Pakistan	0.261	0.826
Argentina	-0.111	0.312	Grenada	-0.371	0.269	Palau	-0.063	0.305
Australia	-0.175	0.400	Guatemala	-0.279	0.332	Panama	-0.232	0.214
Austria	-0.002	0.432	Guinea	-0.187	0.209	Papua New Guinea	-0.094	0.189
Bahamas, The	-0.071	0.219	Guinea-Bissau	-0.147	0.139	Paraguay	-0.349	0.613
Bahrain	0.166	0.332	Guyana	0.305	0.428	Peru	-3.590	2.473
Bangladesh	0.296	0.406	Haiti	-0.824	0.874	Philippines	0.072	0.446
Barbados	-0.024	0.334	Honduras	0.217	0.456	Poland	0.030	0.450
Belgium	-1.055	3.223	Hong Kong SAR, China	-0.596	0.568	Portugal	0.134	0.200
Belize	0.118	0.705	Hungary	-0.360	0.423	Puerto Rico	0.120	0.777
Benin	0.036	0.547	Iceland	-0.298	0.284	Romania	-0.765	0.281
Bermuda	0.023	0.912	India	0.623	0.597	Rwanda	-0.467	0.436
Bhutan	1.033	0.359	Indonesia	0.011	0.462	Samoa	0.700	0.671
Bolivia	-0.744	1.336	Iran, Islamic Rep.	-0.438	0.446	São Tomé and Príncipe	-0.114	0.181
Botswana	0.226	0.263	Iraq	-1.903	0.594	Senegal	-0.051	0.397
Brazil	-0.713	3.293	Ireland	-0.385	0.199	Seychelles	0.222	0.412
Brunei Darussalam	-0.309	0.153	Israel	-0.006	0.153	Sierra Leone	-0.097	0.192
Bulgaria	-0.019	0.080	Italy	-1.521	2.453	Singapore	-1.882	0.980

(continued on next page)

TABLE B.12: **Economic Growth Regressions** *(continued)*

Country	Coefficient	Standard error	Country	Coefficient	Standard error	Country	Coefficient	Standard error
Burkina Faso	-0.155	1.195	Jamaica	-0.859	0.537	Solomon Islands	-0.729	0.464
Burundi	0.310	0.239	Japan	-0.865	1.042	Somalia	-4.655	3.615
Cabo Verde	-0.932	0.987	Korea, Republic of	-0.665	0.277	St. Kitts and Nevis	-0.345	1.310
Cambodia	0.636	0.167	Jordan	-0.050	0.239	South Africa	0.611	1.337
Cameroon	0.147	1.348	Kenya	0.157	0.818	Spain	0.266	0.384
Canada	-0.157	0.567	Kiribati	-0.216	0.396	Sri Lanka	-0.486	2.041
Central African Republic	0.518	0.437	Lao PDR	0.893	0.473	St. Lucia	-0.576	0.990
Chad	-0.398	0.244	Lebanon	0.203	0.356	St. Vincent and the Grenadines	-1.060	0.991
Chile	-0.478	0.174	Lesotho	0.364	0.395	Sudan	-0.203	0.173
China, version 1	1.966	0.526	Liberia	0.505	0.543	Suriname	-0.010	0.079
China, version 2	-10.356	2.636	Luxembourg	-0.183	0.187	Swaziland	-0.240	0.166
Colombia	-0.032	0.138	Macao SAR, China	-0.137	0.240	Sweden	0.127	0.633
Comoros	0.654	0.260	Madagascar	0.171	0.774	Switzerland	0.227	0.711
Congo, Dem. Rep.	-0.192	0.090	Malawi	-0.242	0.158	Syrian Arab Republic	-0.249	0.299
Congo, Republic of	-0.824	0.396	Malaysia	-0.365	0.510	Taiwan, China	-0.598	0.281
Costa Rica	-0.123	0.266	Maldives	0.341	0.210	Tanzania	0.388	0.368
Côte d'Ivoire	0.216	0.458	Mali	0.149	0.213	Thailand	-0.897	1.429

(continued on next page)

TABLE B.12: **Economic Growth Regressions** *(continued)*

Country	Coefficient	Standard error	Country	Coefficient	Standard error	Country	Coefficient	Standard error
Cuba	0.484	0.820	Malta	0.011	0.333	Togo	0.425	0.342
Cyprus	2.552	1.778	Marshall Islands	0.090	0.294	Tonga	0.287	2.785
Denmark	0.184	0.733	Mauritania	−0.062	0.230	Trinidad and Tobago	−0.519	0.211
Djibouti	−0.173	0.372	Mauritius	−1.008	0.570	Tunisia	0.043	0.460
Dominica	−0.422	0.581	Mexico	−0.021	0.425	Turkey	0.101	0.456
Dominican Republic	0.884	0.699	Micronesia, Fed. Sts.	3.778	4.628	Uganda	−0.302	0.555
Ecuador	−0.053	0.323	Mongolia	−0.004	0.410	United Kingdom	−0.293	0.403
Egypt, Arab Rep.	−0.384	0.253	Morocco	−0.216	0.469	United States	−0.024	0.447
El Salvador	0.254	0.508	Mozambique	0.032	0.482	Uruguay	−0.324	3.250
Equatorial Guinea	−0.664	0.062	Namibia	−0.372	0.769	Vanuatu	0.087	0.116
Ethiopia	0.222	0.349	Nepal	0.431	0.455	Venezuela, RB	0.224	0.590
Fiji	0.011	0.420	Netherlands	−0.220	1.133	Vietnam	−2.749	1.184
Finland	1.071	1.440	New Zealand	−0.126	0.679	Zambia	−0.211	0.150
France	0.321	1.249	Nicaragua	−0.428	0.169	Zimbabwe	0.420	0.328
						Mean (Median)	−0.192 (−0.063)	
			Panel E: Infrastructure					
Afghanistan	1.146	0.178	Fiji	−0.011	0.051	Norway	0.190	0.128
Albania	0.129	0.033	Finland	0.027	0.144	Oman	0.121	0.034

(continued on next page)

TABLE B.12: **Economic Growth Regressions** (*continued*)

Country	Coefficient	Standard error	Country	Coefficient	Standard error	Country	Coefficient	Standard error
Algeria	−0.015	0.046	France	−0.013	0.102	Pakistan	0.084	0.038
Angola	0.429	0.112	Gambia, The	−0.081	0.037	Papua New Guinea	0.098	0.237
Antigua and Barbuda	0.169	0.030	Ghana	0.073	0.049	Paraguay	−0.031	0.053
Argentina	0.025	0.061	Greece	0.021	0.090	Peru	0.027	0.045
Australia	0.310	0.162	Grenada	0.160	0.040	Philippines	0.007	0.042
Austria	0.169	0.139	Guatemala	−0.036	0.033	Poland	0.124	0.040
Bahamas, The	0.105	0.074	Guyana	0.069	0.037	Portugal	0.147	0.052
Bahrain	−0.370	0.092	Honduras	−0.031	0.030	Puerto Rico	0.205	0.076
Bangladesh	0.126	0.040	Hong Kong SAR, China	0.410	0.088	Romania	0.110	0.063
Barbados	−0.018	0.055	Hungary	0.043	0.037	Rwanda	−0.047	0.060
Belgium	0.169	0.107	Iceland	−0.001	0.132	São Tomé and Príncipe	−0.068	0.067
Belize	0.146	0.049	India	0.159	0.028	Senegal	0.004	0.036
Benin	−0.001	0.044	Indonesia	0.072	0.024	Seychelles	0.090	0.043
Bermuda	0.147	0.090	Iran, Islamic Rep.	−0.015	0.030	Singapore	0.306	0.100
Bhutan	0.181	0.026	Ireland	0.254	0.057	South Africa	−0.072	0.116
Botswana	0.127	0.033	Israel	0.139	0.094	Spain	0.142	0.083
Brazil	−0.031	0.043	Italy	0.184	0.113	Sri Lanka	0.102	0.026
Burkina Faso	0.016	0.033	Jamaica	−0.001	0.037	St. Lucia	0.166	0.037

(continued on next page)

TABLE B.12: **Economic Growth Regressions** *(continued)*

Country	Coefficient	Standard error	Country	Coefficient	Standard error	Country	Coefficient	Standard error
Burundi	−0.177	0.046	Japan	0.436	0.179	St. Vincent and the Grenadines	0.248	0.043
Cabo Verde	0.105	0.023	Lao PDR	0.179	0.032	Swaziland	0	0.051
Cameroon	−0.223	0.052	Kenya	−0.042	0.105	Sudan	0.107	0.040
Canada	0.211	0.160	Korea, Republic of	0.250	0.042	Suriname	−0.093	0.055
Chad	0.109	0.038	Lesotho	0.071	0.049	Sweden	0.155	0.368
Chile	0.234	0.037	Luxembourg	0.748	0.141	Switzerland	0.065	0.153
China	0.213	0.019	Malawi	−0.096	0.064	Syrian Arab Republic	−0.033	0.044
Colombia	0.035	0.047	Malaysia	0.169	0.037	Tanzania	0.247	0.102
Comoros	−0.138	0.034	Mali	0.086	0.034	Thailand	0.174	0.028
Congo, Dem. Rep.	0.382	0.069	Malta	0.214	0.065	Trinidad and Tobago	−0.026	0.052
Congo, Republic of	0.156	0.096	Mauritania	−0.016	0.033	Tunisia	0.056	0.035
Costa Rica	0.031	0.044	Mauritius	0.162	0.030	Turkey	0.078	0.030
Côte d'Ivoire	−0.193	0.061	Mexico	−0.007	0.054	Uganda	0.220	0.073
Cyprus	0.200	0.054	Morocco	0.062	0.036	United Kingdom	0.368	0.107
Denmark	0.312	0.161	Mozambique	0.396	0.192	United States	0.412	0.186
Djibouti	−0.570	0.322	Namibia	−0.002	0.113	Uruguay	0.129	0.050
Dominica	0.153	0.035	Nepal	0.070	0.024	Vanuatu	0.001	0.061
Ecuador	−0.026	0.046	Netherlands	0.199	0.137	Venezuela, RB	−0.104	0.065

(continued on next page)

137

TABLE B.12: **Economic Growth Regressions** *(continued)*

Country	Coefficient	Standard error	Country	Coefficient	Standard error	Country	Coefficient	Standard error
Egypt, Arab Rep.	0.178	0.032	New Zealand	0.341	0.270	Zambia	0.075	0.206
El Salvador	0.028	0.030	Nicaragua	-0.147	0.053	Zimbabwe	-0.507	0.095
Ethiopia	0.086	0.053	Niger	-0.268	0.073	Mean (Median)	0.095 (0.088)	
			Panel F: Political institutions					
Albania	0.008	0.008	France	-0.042	0.121	Nicaragua	-0.012	0.009
Algeria	-0.011	0.013	Gabon	-0.046	0.024	Niger	-0.008	0.009
Angola	0.059	0.023	Gambia, The	0.016	0.009	Nigeria	-0.026	0.037
Argentina	0.008	0.020	Ghana	0.012	0.011	Norway	0.143	0.017
Australia	0.134	0.017	Greece	-0.015	0.019	Oman	-0.027	0.057
Austria	0.135	0.017	Guatemala	-0.008	0.013	Pakistan	-0.003	0.012
Bahrain	0.037	0.041	Guinea	-0.010	0.013	Panama	0.003	0.009
Bangladesh	0.005	0.010	Guinea-Bissau	-0.023	0.010	Papua New Guinea	0.126	0.023
Belgium	0.074	0.139	Guyana	0.017	0.009	Paraguay	-0.014	0.009
Benin	-0.012	0.010	Haiti	-0.013	0.008	Peru	0.010	0.014
Bhutan	0.026	0.035	Honduras	-0.024	0.024	Philippines	-0.008	0.015
Bolivia	-0.001	0.012	Hungary	0.006	0.008	Poland	0.011	0.009
Botswana	-0.001	0.061	India	0.239	0.126	Portugal	0.003	0.019
Brazil	-0.013	0.012	Indonesia	0.002	0.009	Romania	0.002	0.008

(continued on next page)

TABLE B.12: **Economic Growth Regressions** *(continued)*

Country	Coefficient	Standard error	Country	Coefficient	Standard error	Country	Coefficient	Standard error
Bulgaria	0.001	0.009	Iran, Islamic Rep.	0.069	0.039	Rwanda	0.022	0.028
Burkina Faso	−0.001	0.022	Ireland	0.130	0.016	São Tomé and Príncipe	0.018	0.070
Burundi	−0.027	0.010	Israel	−0.041	0.138	Senegal	−0.032	0.008
Cameroon	−0.045	0.030	Italy	0.129	0.016	Singapore	0.009	0.011
Canada	0.134	0.017	Jamaica	0.157	0.117	South Africa	0	0.016
Central African Republic	−0.035	0.015	Japan	0.132	0.016	Spain	−0.008	0.024
Chad	−0.053	0.037	Jordan	−0.018	0.016	Sri Lanka	0.023	0.015
Chile	0.019	0.009	Kenya	−0.007	0.008	St. Kitts and Nevis	−0.133	0.068
China	0.876	0.361	Korea, Republic of	0.017	0.011	Sweden	−0.065	0.094
Colombia	0.058	0.109	Lao PDR	−0.084	0.112	Switzerland	0.136	0.018
Comoros	−0.033	0.010	Lesotho	0.005	0.008	Syrian Arab Republic	0.065	0.010
Congo, Dem. Rep.	−0.035	0.010	Liberia	−0.022	0.014	Tanzania	0.032	0.025
Congo, Republic of	−0.116	0.031	Madagascar	−0.024	0.013	Thailand	0.012	0.010
Costa Rica	0.095	0.013	Malawi	−0.003	0.008	Togo	−0.061	0.032
Côte d'Ivoire	−0.018	0.009	Malaysia	−0.047	0.136	Tunisia	0.004	0.020
Cyprus	−0.161	0.020	Mali	−0.003	0.008	Turkey	0.012	0.029
Denmark	0.132	0.017	Mauritania	0.001	0.019	Uganda	−0.008	0.022
Dominican Republic	0.013	0.025	Mauritius	0.534	0.270	United Kingdom	0.130	0.016

(continued on next page)

TABLE B.12: **Economic Growth Regressions** *(continued)*

Country	Coefficient	Standard error	Country	Coefficient	Standard error	Country	Coefficient	Standard error
Ecuador	−0.010	0.014	Mexico	−0.008	0.008	United States	0.137	0.017
Egypt, Arab Rep.	0.036	0.040	Mongolia	−0.002	0.008	Uruguay	0.014	0.014
El Salvador	0.003	0.020	Morocco	0.028	0.052	Venezuela, RB	0.024	0.029
Equatorial Guinea	0.598	0.068	Mozambique	0.021	0.008	Zambia	0.007	0.009
Ethiopia	0.007	0.014	Nepal	0.008	0.015	Zimbabwe	0.019	0.022
Fiji	0.008	0.013	Netherlands	0.134	0.017	Mean (Median)	0.034 (0.005)	
Finland	0.130	0.016	New Zealand	0.123	0.016			
Panel G: Lack of price stability								
Algeria	−0.043	0.246	Gabon	−0.009	0.147	Norway	0.013	0.409
Argentina	−0.019	0.034	Gambia, The	0.102	0.140	Pakistan	−0.039	0.303
Australia	0.001	0.306	Ghana	−1.090	1.376	Panama	0.175	0.146
Austria	−0.047	0.278	Greece	−0.041	0.123	Papua New Guinea	−0.134	0.249
Bahamas, The	0.050	0.094	Guatemala	−0.046	0.131	Paraguay	0.068	0.140
Bangladesh	−0.254	0.277	Guinea-Bissau	0.085	0.072	Peru	−0.022	0.029
Barbados	−0.028	0.106	Guyana	−0.088	0.077	Philippines	−0.090	0.268
Belgium	−0.052	0.333	Honduras	0	0.378	Portugal	0.109	0.110

(continued on next page)

TABLE B.12: **Economic Growth Regressions** *(continued)*

Country	Coefficient	Standard error	Country	Coefficient	Standard error	Country	Coefficient	Standard error
Belize	−0.042	0.255	Hungary	0.008	0.118	Puerto Rico	−0.580	0.342
Benin	−0.028	0.174	Iceland	0.134	0.211	Rwanda	0.086	0.115
Bermuda	0.006	0.223	India	−0.520	0.455	Senegal	−0.027	0.232
Bolivia	−0.054	0.106	Indonesia	0.062	0.210	Seychelles	−0.092	0.180
Botswana	0.057	0.392	Iran, Islamic Rep.	0.043	0.242	Sierra Leone	0.103	0.094
Brazil	0.020	0.039	Israel	0.030	0.070	Singapore	−0.274	0.244
Burkina Faso	0.047	0.215	Italy	0.089	0.130	South Africa	−0.195	0.297
Burundi	−0.280	0.120	Jamaica	0.295	0.402	Spain	0.029	0.147
Cameroon	0.044	0.134	Kenya	0.118	0.225	Sri Lanka	−5.271	5.920
Canada	−0.043	0.136	Kiribati	0.727	0.666	St. Vincent and the Grenadines	−0.225	0.175
Central African Republic	−0.124	0.188	Korea, Republic of	0.040	0.204	Sudan	−0.076	0.128
Chad	0.031	0.050	Lesotho	−0.133	0.405	Swaziland	0.500	0.325
Chile	−0.160	0.072	Liberia	−0.095	0.049	Sweden	−0.056	0.125
China version 1	0.410	0.126	Luxembourg	−0.170	0.310	Syrian Arab Republic	−0.089	0.142
Colombia	−0.023	0.132	Madagascar	0.264	0.359	Thailand	−0.073	0.503
Congo, Dem. Rep.	−0.047	0.044	Malawi	−0.256	0.177	Togo	−0.592	0.596
Costa Rica	−0.151	0.360	Malaysia	0.224	0.292	Trinidad and Tobago	−0.121	0.350

(continued on next page)

TABLE B.12: Economic Growth Regressions *(continued)*

Country	Coefficient	Standard error	Country	Coefficient	Standard error	Country	Coefficient	Standard error
Cuba	−0.046	0.193	Malta	−0.021	0.252	Tunisia	−0.008	0.211
Denmark	−0.015	0.141	Mauritania	−0.127	0.269	Turkey	−0.016	0.097
Dominican Republic	−0.148	0.115	Mexico	−0.031	0.079	United Kingdom	−0.068	0.125
Egypt, Arab Rep.	−0.006	0.429	Morocco	−0.067	0.126	United States	−0.076	0.211
El Salvador	0.008	0.512	Nepal	0.069	0.334	Uruguay	0.009	0.077
Fiji	−0.081	0.268	Netherlands	0.065	0.215	Venezuela, RB	−0.044	0.479
Finland	−0.004	0.099	Nicaragua	−0.002	0.035	Zambia	−0.073	0.093
France	0.037	0.184	Nigeria	−0.291	0.177	Mean (Median)	−0.089 (−0.027)	

Panel H: Real exchange rate

Country	Coefficient	Standard error	Country	Coefficient	Standard error	Country	Coefficient	Standard error
Algeria	0.063	0.374	Gabon	0.221	0.377	Norway	−0.265	0.322
Argentina	−0.141	0.175	Gambia, The	0.118	0.107	Pakistan	−0.190	0.234
Australia	−0.752	0.515	Ghana	−0.100	0.059	Panama	−0.226	0.378
Austria	−0.126	0.280	Greece	0.034	0.220	Papua New Guinea	−0.004	0.138
Bahamas, The	−1.361	0.491	Guatemala	−0.258	0.404	Paraguay	1.097	0.542
Bangladesh	−0.475	0.379	Guinea-Bissau	0.155	0.088	Peru	0.101	0.211
Barbados	0.053	0.201	Guyana	0.029	0.269	Philippines	0.677	0.848
Belgium	−0.100	0.272	Honduras	0.211	0.362	Portugal	−0.137	0.194
Belize	−0.331	0.933	Hungary	−0.075	0.155	Puerto Rico	−0.720	0.786

(continued on next page)

TABLE B.12: Economic Growth Regressions *(continued)*

Country	Coefficient	Standard error	Country	Coefficient	Standard error	Country	Coefficient	Standard error
Benin	−0.531	0.306	Iceland	−0.338	0.270	Rwanda	−0.700	0.666
Bermuda	0.181	0.280	India	−0.319	0.164	Senegal	−0.180	0.283
Bolivia	−0.152	0.303	Indonesia	−0.083	0.199	Seychelles	−1.113	1.182
Botswana	−0.475	0.561	Iran, Islamic Rep.	−0.638	0.217	Sierra Leone	0.086	0.199
Brazil	−0.083	0.161	Israel	0.282	0.462	Singapore	0.195	0.601
Burkina Faso	−0.024	0.240	Italy	−0.343	0.264	South Africa	−0.747	1.104
Burundi	0.278	0.102	Jamaica	−0.359	0.298	Spain	−0.084	0.224
Cameroon	0.395	0.270	Kenya	0.021	0.191	Sri Lanka	−0.185	0.459
Canada	−0.792	0.738	Kiribati	0.516	0.422	St. Vincent and the Grenadines	1.119	0.427
Central African Republic	0.092	0.186	Korea, Republic of	−0.331	0.479	Sudan	0.045	0.200
Chad	−0.444	0.245	Lesotho	0.791	1.675	Swaziland	−0.068	0.298
Chile	−0.630	0.437	Liberia	0.480	0.280	Sweden	−0.261	0.386
China version 1	−0.392	0.118	Luxembourg	−0.126	0.262	Syrian Arab Republic	0.107	0.173
Colombia	0.418	1.376	Madagascar	0.010	0.325	Thailand	−0.882	0.815
Congo, Dem. Rep.	−0.346	0.137	Malawi	−0.033	0.257	Togo	0.318	0.351
Costa Rica	0.374	0.294	Malaysia	−0.064	0.247	Trinidad and Tobago	−0.368	0.358
Cuba	−0.400	0.266	Malta	0.023	0.523	Tunisia	0.155	0.394
Denmark	−0.275	0.282	Mauritania	0.064	0.112	Turkey	0.060	0.245

(continued on next page)

143

TABLE B.12: **Economic Growth Regressions** *(continued)*

Country	Coefficient	Standard error	Country	Coefficient	Standard error	Country	Coefficient	Standard error
Dominican Republic	−0.129	0.403	Mexico	−0.334	0.408	United Kingdom	−0.438	0.527
Egypt, Arab Rep.	0.075	0.213	Morocco	0.148	0.353	United States	−0.087	0.150
El Salvador	0.053	0.064	Nepal	−0.118	0.260	Uruguay	0.694	0.622
Fiji	0.159	0.288	Netherlands	−0.027	0.292	Venezuela	−0.215	0.244
Finland	−0.535	0.429	Nicaragua	−0.400	0.286	Zambia	−0.266	0.160
France	−0.293	0.341	Nigeria	−0.378	0.191	Mean (Median)	−0.106 (−0.093)	

TABLE B.13: **Economic Growth Regressions (10-Year Panels)**

				Dependent variable: ln(GDP p.c.)					
	(1)	(2)	(3)	(4)	(5)	(6)	(7)	(8)	(9)
Variable	SYS GMM	SYS GMM	SYS GMM	SYS GMM	SYS GMM	SYS GMM	SYS GMM	SYS GMM	SYS GMM
ln(GDP p.c.), $t-1$	0.66*** (0.05)	0.71*** (0.04)	0.72*** (0.03)	0.72*** (0.03)	0.65*** (0.03)	0.73*** (0.05)	0.72*** (0.04)	0.73*** (0.04)	0.72*** (0.04)
ln(secondary school enrollment rate), t	0.13*** (0.04)								
ln(private domestic credit/GDP), t		0.11*** (0.03)							
ln(structure adjusted trade volume/GDP), t			0.15*** (0.04)						
ln(government consumption/ GDP), t				−0.25*** (0.05)					
ln(telephone lines p.c.), t					0.17*** (0.02)				
Polity2 score, t						−0.01 (0.01)			
Inflation rate, t							−0.14*** (0.03)		
ln(real exchange rate), t								−0.03* (0.01)	
Banking crisis, t									−0.11* (0.06)
AR (1) test, p-value	0.01	0.03	0.00	0.00	0.00	0.00	0.01	0.00	0.00

(continued on next page)

TABLE B.13: **Economic Growth Regressions (10-Year Panels)** *(continued)*

Variable	(1) SYS GMM	(2) SYS GMM	(3) SYS GMM	(4) SYS GMM	Dependent variable: ln(GDP p.c.) (5) SYS GMM	(6) SYS GMM	(7) SYS GMM	(8) SYS GMM	(9) SYS GMM
AR (2) test, p-value	0.31	0.13	0.61	0.58	0.36	0.33	0.51	0.33	0.35
Country FE	Yes	Yes	Yes	Yes	Yes	Yes	Yes	Yes	Yes
Year FE	Yes	Yes	Yes	Yes	Yes	Yes	Yes	Yes	Yes
Observations	661	681	795	795	743	633	707	795	795
Countries	184	178	190	190	186	155	186	190	190

Note: The dependent variable is real GDP per capita. The method of estimation is system-GMM (system–general method of moments). FE = fixed effects; GDP = gross domestic product; p.c. = per capita; SYS GMM = system–general method of moments; t = time.

*Significantly different from zero at the 10 percent significance level, ** 5 percent significance level, *** 1 percent significance level.

TABLE B.14: Growth Predictions for 2011–20 under a Scenario of Continuous Trends

Country	Change in log GDP p.c. 2001–2010	Projected change in log GDP p.c. 2011–2020	Change in log projected change									
			Persistence	Education	Financial development	Trade openness	Government burden	Infrastructure	Inflation	Real exchange rate	Banking crisis	External conditions
Argentina	0.326	0.298	0.198	0.000	0.000	0.020	0.036	0.034	-0.002	-0.003	0.005	0.010
Bolivia	0.183	0.174	0.111	-0.002	-0.033	0.005	0.012	0.061	-0.002	-0.007	0.000	0.029
Brazil	0.197	0.183	0.120	0.001	0.036	0.032	0.002	-0.005	0.004	-0.025	0.000	0.018
Chile	0.294	0.263	0.179	0.000	-0.002	0.021	0.022	-0.009	0.003	-0.016	0.000	0.065
Colombia	0.262	0.191	0.159	0.006	0.009	0.024	0.006	-0.026	0.004	-0.004	0.000	0.013
Costa Rica	0.260	0.400	0.158	0.013	0.057	0.001	0.132	0.041	0.000	0.000	0.000	-0.002
Dominican Republic	0.367	0.182	0.223	0.003	-0.026	-0.024	0.009	-0.009	0.008	-0.007	0.006	-0.001
Ecuador	0.297	0.260	0.181	0.003	0.000	0.003	-0.006	0.058	0.002	-0.006	0.006	0.019
El Salvador	0.147	0.214	0.089	0.002	0.002	0.004	0.017	0.107	0.000	-0.010	0.000	0.003
Guatemala	0.125	0.175	0.076	0.010	0.015	-0.012	-0.021	0.108	-0.004	-0.004	0.000	0.007
Guyana	0.348	0.288	0.212	0.000	-0.053	0.008	0.002	0.158	-0.009	-0.020	0.000	-0.010
Haiti	0.017	-0.056	0.010	0.008	0.001	0.007	-0.001	-0.052	-0.005	-0.012	0.000	-0.012
Honduras	0.179	0.397	0.109	0.001	0.029	-0.016	-0.005	0.273	0.001	-0.007	0.008	0.004
Jamaica	-0.024	-0.159	-0.015	0.002	0.006	0.005	-0.020	-0.108	0.000	-0.005	0.000	-0.024
Mexico	0.048	0.135	0.029	0.003	0.009	0.021	0.021	0.045	0.008	-0.002	0.000	0.001

(continued on next page)

147

TABLE B.14: Growth Predictions for 2011–20 under a Scenario of Continuous Trends *(continued)*

Country	Change in log GDP p.c. 2001–2010	Projected change in log GDP p.c. 2011–2020	Change in log projected change									
			Persistence	Education	Financial development	Trade openness	Government burden	Infrastructure	Inflation	Real exchange rate	Banking crisis	External conditions
Nicaragua	0.103	0.228	0.063	0.003	0.010	0.025	0.009	0.089	−0.003	−0.001	0.018	0.015
Panama	0.445	0.472	0.271	0.002	−0.003	0.003	0.158	0.046	−0.002	0.001	0.000	−0.004
Paraguay	0.213	0.201	0.130	0.001	0.008	0.017	−0.010	0.045	0.003	−0.008	0.005	0.010
Peru	0.439	0.451	0.267	0.000	0.002	0.007	0.007	0.145	−0.002	−0.011	0.000	0.036
Uruguay	0.307	0.204	0.187	−0.005	−0.024	0.033	0.017	−0.004	0.006	−0.007	−0.003	0.004
Venezuela, RB	0.049	0.302	0.030	0.007	0.081	−0.005	−0.026	0.212	0.003	−0.022	0.000	0.022
Mean	0.218	0.229	0.133	0.003	0.006	0.009	0.017	0.058	0.001	−0.008	0.002	0.010

Note: The predictions are generated based on the estimates reported in column 2 in Table B.4 and forecasts for changes in the determinants of growth obtained from univariate time-series models. To convert numbers into annual changes, all values have to be divided by 10. GDP = gross domestic product; p.c. = per capita.

*Significantly different from zero at the 10 percent significance level, ** 5 percent significance level, *** 1 percent significance level.

TABLE B.15: Growth Predictions with Roads as a Proxy for Infrastructure

Country	Change in log GDP per capita 2001–2010	Projected change in log GDP per capita 2011–2020	Contributions to projected change									
			Persistence	Education	Financial development	Trade openness	Government burden	Roads	Inflation	Real exchange rate	Banking crisis	External conditions
Argentina	0.326	0.281	0.198	0.000	0.000	0.020	0.036	0.017	-0.002	-0.003	0.005	0.010
Bolivia	0.183	0.141	0.111	-0.002	-0.033	0.005	0.012	0.028	-0.002	-0.007	0.000	0.029
Brazil	0.197	0.139	0.120	0.001	0.036	0.032	0.002	-0.049	0.004	-0.025	0.000	0.018
Chile	0.294	0.223	0.179	0.000	-0.002	0.021	0.022	-0.049	0.003	-0.016	0.000	0.065
Colombia	0.242	0.148	0.159	0.006	0.0009	0.024	0.006	-0.069	0.004	-0.004	0.000	0.013
Costa Rica	0.260	0.281	0.158	0.013	0.057	0.001	0.132	-0.078	0.000	0.000	0.000	-0.002
Dominican Republic	0.367	0.168	0.223	0.003	-0.026	-0.024	0.009	-0.023	0.008	-0.007	0.006	-0.001
Ecuador	0.297	0.129	0.181	0.003	0.000	0.003	-0.006	-0.073	0.002	-0.006	0.006	0.019
El Salvador	0.147	-0.029	0.089	0.002	0.002	0.004	0.017	-0.136	0.000	-0.010	0.000	0.003
Guatemala	0.125	0.041	0.076	0.010	0.015	-0.012	-0.021	-0.026	-0.004	-0.004	0.000	0.007
Guyana	0.348	0.172	0.212	0.000	-0.053	0.008	0.002	0.042	-0.009	-0.020	0.000	-0.010
Haiti	0.017	-0.041	0.010	0.008	0.001	0.007	-0.001	-0.037	-0.005	-0.012	0.000	-0.012
Honduras	0.175	0.080	0.109	0.001	0.029	-0.016	-0.005	-0.044	0.001	-0.007	0.008	0.004
Jamaica	-0.024	-0.034	-0.015	0.002	0.006	0.005	-0.020	0.017	0.000	-0.005	0.000	-0.024
Mexico	0.048	0.118	0.029	0.003	0.009	0.021	0.021	0.028	0.008	-0.002	0.000	0.001

(continued on next page)

149

TABLE B.15: **Growth Predictions with Roads as a Proxy for Infrastructure** *(continued)*

Country	Change in log GDP per capita 2001–2010	Projected change in log GDP per capita 2011–2020	Contributions to projected change									
			Persistence	Education	Financial development	Trade openness	Government burden	Roads	Inflation	Real exchange rate	Banking crisis	External conditions
Nicaragua	0.103	0.114	0.063	0.003	0.010	0.025	0.009	−0.025	−0.003	−0.001	0.018	0.018
Panama	0.445	0.419	0.271	0.002	−0.003	0.003	0.158	−0.007	−0.002	0.001	0.000	−0.004
Paraguay	0.213	0.095	0.130	0.001	0.008	0.017	−0.010	−0.061	0.003	−0.006	0.005	0.010
Peru	0.439	0.327	0.267	0.000	0.002	0.007	0.007	0.021	−0.002	−0.011	0.000	0.036
Uruguay	0.307	0.208	0.187	−0.005	−0.024	0.033	0.017	0.000	0.006	−0.007	−0.003	0.004
Venezuela, RB	0.049	0.104	0.030	0.007	0.081	−0.005	−0.026	0.014	0.003	−0.022	0.000	0.022
Mean	0.218	0.147	0.133	0.003	0.006	0.009	0.017	−0.024	0.001	−0.008	0.002	0.010

Note: The predictions are generated based on the estimates reported in column (1) of Table 5. To convert numbers into per annum changes, all values have to be divided by 10. *Significantly different from zero at the 10 percent significance level, ** 5 percent significance level, *** 1 percent significance level.

TABLE B.16: **Growth Predictions with Composite Index as a Proxy for Infrastructure**

Country	Change in log GDP p.c. 2001–2010	Projected change in log GDP p.c. 2011–2020	Contributions to projected change									
			Persistence	Education	Financial development	Trade openness	Government burden	Infrastructure index	Inflation	Real exchange rate	Banking crisi	External conditions
Argentina	0.326	0.275	0.199	0.000	0.000	0.020	0.036	0.011	-0.002	-0.003	0.005	0.010
Bolivia	0.183	0.123	0.111	-0.002	-0.033	0.005	0.012	0.011	-0.002	-0.007	0.000	0.029
Brazil	0.197	0.209	0.120	0.001	0.036	0.032	0.002	0.022	0.004	-0.025	0.000	0.018
Chile	0.294	0.286	0.179	0.000	-0.002	0.021	0.022	0.012	0.003	-0.016	0.000	0.065
Colombia	0.262	0.223	0.160	0.006	0.009	0.024	0.006	0.004	0.004	-0.004	0.000	0.013
Costa Rica	0.260	0.373	0.158	0.013	0.057	0.001	0.132	0.015	0.000	0.000	0.000	-0.002
Dominican Republic	0.367	0.433	0.223	0.003	-0.026	-0.024	0.009	0.242	0.008	-0.007	0.006	-0.001
Ecuador	0.297	0.214	0.180	0.003	0.000	0.003	-0.006	0.013	0.002	-0.006	0.006	0.019
El Salvador	0.147	0.295	0.089	0.002	0.002	0.004	0.017	0.187	0.000	-0.010	0.000	0.003
Guatemala	0.125	0.256	0.076	0.010	0.015	-0.012	-0.021	0.189	-0.004	-0.004	0.000	0.007
Guyana	0.348	0.232	0.212	0.000	-0.053	0.008	0.002	0.103	-0.009	-0.020	0.000	-0.010
Haiti	0.017	0.051	0.010	0.008	0.001	0.007	-0.001	0.055	-0.005	-0.012	0.000	-0.012
Honduras	0.179	0.425	0.109	0.001	0.029	-0.016	-0.005	0.302	0.001	-0.007	0.008	0.004
Jamaica	-0.024	-0.047	-0.014	0.002	0.006	0.005	-0.020	0.002	0.000	-0.005	0.000	-0.024
Mexico	0.048	0.108	0.029	0.003	0.009	0.021	0.021	0.018	0.008	-0.002	0.000	0.001

(continued on next page)

TABLE B.16: **Growth Predictions with Composite Index as a Proxy for Infrastructure** (continued)

Country	Change in log GDP p.c. 2001–2010	Projected change in log GDP p.c. 2011–2020	Contributions to projected change									
			Persistence	Education	Financial development	Trade openness	Government burden	Infrastructure index	Inflation	Real exchange rate	Banking crisi	External conditions
Nicaragua	0.103	0.141	0.063	0.003	0.010	0.025	0.009	0.001	-0.003	-0.001	0.018	0.015
Panama	0.445	0.426	0.271	0.002	-0.003	0.003	0.158	0.000	-0.002	0.001	0.000	-0.004
Paraguay	0.213	0.155	0.130	0.001	0.008	0.017	-0.010	0.001	0.003	-0.008	0.005	0.010
Peru	0.439	0.314	0.267	0.000	0.002	0.007	0.007	0.009	-0.002	-0.011	0.000	0.036
Uruguay	0.307	0.136	0.187	-0.005	-0.024	0.033	0.017	-0.073	0.006	-0.007	-0.003	0.004
Venezuela, RB	0.049	0.213	0.030	0.007	0.081	-0.005	-0.026	0.125	0.003	-0.022	0.000	0.022
LAC Mean	0.218	0.231	0.133	0.003	0.006	0.009	0.017	0.059	0.001	-0.008	0.002	0.010

TABLE B.17: **Economic Growth Regressions**
(conditional effects, five-year unbalanced panel)

	Dependent variable: ln(GDP p.c.)	
Variable	(1) SYS GMM	(2) LS
ln(GDP p.c.), $t-1$	0.81***	0.78***
	(0.05)	(0.03)
Structural policies and institutions		
ln(secondary school enrollment rate), t	0.02	−0.01
	(0.05)	(0.03)
ln(private domestic credit/GDP), t	0.08***	0.03
	(0.03)	(0.02)
ln(structure adjusted trade volume/GDP), t	0.11**	0.12***
	(0.05)	(0.03)
ln(government consumption/GDP), t	−0.30***	−0.13***
	(0.04)	(0.03)
Infrastructure index, t	0.08***	0.06***
	(0.02)	(0.02)
Polity2 score, t	0.01	−0.01
	(0.03)	(0.02)
Stabilization policies		
Inflation rate, t	−0.01	−0.01
	(0.01)	(0.01)
ln(real exchange rate), t	−0.06	−0.02
	(0.04)	(0.03)
Banking crisis, t	−0.05*	−0.06**
	(0.03)	(0.03)
External conditions		
ComPI growth, t	7.81***	5.78**
	(2.63)	(2.58)
Terms-of-trade growth, t	0.14***	0.12***
	(0.03)	(0.03)
AR (1) test, p-value	0.02	−
AR (2) test, p-value	0.03	−
Sargan test $\chi^2(10)$, p-value	0.03	−
Country FE	Yes	Yes
Year FE	Yes	Yes
Observations	464	464
Countries	126	126

Note: The dependent variable is real GDP per capita. The method of estimation in column (1) is system-GMM (system–general method of moments); column (2) least squares. The system-GMM estimation is based on 10 endogenous variables and 20 instruments. En dashes indicate that these tests were not performed for the least-squares regressions. ComPI = international commodity export price index; FE = fixed effects; GDP = gross domestic product; LS = least squares; p.c. = per capita; SYS GMM = system–general method of moments; t = time.
*Significantly different from zero at the 10 percent significance level, ** 5 percent significance level, *** 1 percent significance level.

TABLE B.18: **Growth Forecasts for 2011–20, Keeping the Commodity Price Index and Terms of Trade at Their 2010 Levels** *(all other variables are under the scenario of continuous trends)*

Country	Change in log GDP p.c. 2001–2010	Projected change in log GDP p.c. 2011–2020	Contributions to projected change									
			Persistence	Education	Financial development	Trade openness	Government burden	Infrastructure	Inflation	Real exchange rate	Banking crisis	External conditions
Argentina	0.326	0.288	0.198	0.000	0.000	0.020	0.036	0.034	-0.002	-0.003	0.005	0.000
Bolivia	0.183	0.145	0.111	-0.002	-0.033	0.005	0.012	0.061	-0.002	-0.007	0.000	0.000
Brazil	0.197	0.165	0.120	0.001	0.036	0.032	0.002	-0.005	0.004	-0.025	0.000	0.000
Chile	0.294	0.198	0.179	0.000	-0.002	0.021	0.022	-0.009	0.003	-0.016	0.000	0.000
Colombia	0.262	0.178	0.159	0.006	0.009	0.024	0.006	-0.026	0.004	-0.004	0.000	0.000
Costa Rica	0.260	0.402	0.158	0.013	0.057	0.001	0.132	0.041	0.000	0.000	0.000	0.000
Dominican Republic	0.367	0.183	0.223	0.003	-0.026	-0.024	0.009	-0.009	0.008	-0.007	0.006	0.000
Ecuador	0.297	0.241	0.181	0.003	0.000	0.003	-0.006	0.058	0.002	-0.006	0.006	0.000
El Salvador	0.147	0.211	0.089	0.002	0.002	0.004	0.017	0.107	0.000	-0.010	0.000	0.000
Guatemala	0.125	0.168	0.076	0.010	0.015	-0.012	-0.021	0.108	-0.004	-0.004	0.000	0.000
Guyana	0.348	0.298	0.212	0.000	-0.053	0.008	0.002	0.158	-0.009	-0.020	0.000	0.000
Haiti	0.017	-0.044	0.010	0.008	0.001	0.007	-0.001	-0.052	-0.005	-0.012	0.000	0.000

(continued on next page)

TABLE B.18: Growth Forecasts for 2011–20, Keeping the Commodity Price Index and Terms of Trade at Their 2010 Levels *(continued)*

Country	Change in log GDP p.c. 2001–2010	Projected change in log GDP p.c. 2011–2020	Contributions to projected change									
			Persistence	Education	Financial development	Trade openness	Government burden	Infrastructure	Inflation	Real exchange rate	Banking crisis	External conditions
Honduras	0.179	0.393	0.109	0.001	0.029	−0.016	−0.005	0.273	0.001	−0.007	0.008	0.000
Jamaica	−0.024	−0.135	−0.015	0.002	0.006	0.005	−0.020	−0.108	0.000	−0.005	0.000	0.000
Mexico	0.048	0.134	0.029	0.003	0.009	0.021	0.021	0.045	0.008	−0.002	0.000	0.000
Nicaragua	0.103	0.213	0.063	0.003	0.010	0.025	0.009	0.089	−0.003	−0.001	0.018	0.000
Panama	0.445	0.476	0.271	0.002	−0.003	0.003	0.158	0.046	−0.002	0.001	0.000	0.000
Paraguay	0.213	0.191	0.130	0.001	0.008	0.017	−0.010	0.045	0.003	−0.008	0.005	0.000
Peru	0.439	0.415	0.267	0.000	0.002	0.007	0.007	0.145	−0.002	−0.011	0.000	0.000
Uruguay	0.307	0.200	0.187	−0.005	−0.024	0.033	0.017	−0.004	0.006	−0.007	−0.003	0.000
Venezuela, RB	0.049	0.280	0.030	0.007	0.081	−0.005	−0.026	0.212	0.003	−0.022	0.000	0.000

TABLE B.10: Growth Forecasts for 2011–20 with a Reversal in External Conditions

Country	Change in log GDP p.c. 2001–2010	Projected change in log GDP p.c. 2011–2020	Contributions to projected change									
			Persistence	Education	Financial development	Trade openness	Government burden	Infrastructure	Inflation	Real exchange rate	Banking crisis	External conditions
Argentina	0.326	0.238	0.199	0.000	0.000	0.020	0.036	0.034	-0.002	-0.003	0.005	-0.050
Bolivia	0.183	0.085	0.111	-0.002	-0.033	0.005	0.012	0.061	-0.002	-0.007	0.000	-0.060
Brazil	0.197	0.155	0.120	0.001	0.036	0.032	0.002	-0.005	0.004	-0.025	0.000	-0.010
Chile	0.294	-0.011	0.179	0.000	-0.002	0.021	0.022	-0.009	0.003	-0.016	0.000	-0.210
Colombia	0.262	0.120	0.160	0.006	0.009	0.024	0.006	-0.026	0.004	-0.004	0.000	-0.060
Costa Rica	0.260	0.421	0.158	0.013	0.057	0.001	0.132	0.041	0.000	0.000	0.000	0.020
Dominican Republic	0.367	0.162	0.223	0.003	-0.026	-0.024	0.009	-0.009	0.008	-0.007	0.006	-0.020
Ecuador	0.297	0.151	0.180	0.003	0.000	0.003	-0.006	0.058	0.002	-0.006	0.006	-0.090
El Salvador	0.147	0.222	0.089	0.002	0.002	0.004	0.017	0.107	0.000	-0.010	0.000	0.010
Guatemala	0.125	0.178	0.076	0.010	0.015	-0.012	-0.021	0.108	-0.004	-0.004	0.000	0.010
Guyana	0.348	0.016	0.212	0.000	-0.053	0.008	0.002	0.158	-0.009	-0.020	0.000	-0.280
Haiti	0.017	-0.013	0.010	0.008	0.001	0.007	-0.001	-0.052	-0.005	-0.012	0.000	0.030
Honduras	0.179	0.402	0.109	0.001	0.029	-0.016	-0.005	0.273	0.001	-0.007	0.008	0.010
Jamaica	-0.024	-0.173	-0.014	0.002	0.006	0.005	-0.020	-0.108	0.000	-0.005	0.000	-0.040
Mexico	0.048	0.094	0.029	0.003	0.009	0.021	0.021	0.045	0.008	-0.002	0.000	-0.040

(continued on next page)

TABLE B.19: Growth Forecasts for 2011–20 with a Reversal in External Conditions *(continued)*

Country	Change in log GDP p.c. 2001–2010	Projected change in log GDP p.c. 2011–2020	Persistence	Education	Financial development	Trade openness	Government burden	Infrastructure	Inflation	Real exchange rate	Banking crisis	External conditions
							Contributions to projected change					
Nicaragua	0.103	0.233	0.063	0.003	0.010	0.025	0.009	0.089	−0.003	−0.001	0.018	0.020
Panama	0.445	0.466	0.271	0.002	−0.003	0.003	0.158	0.046	−0.002	0.001	0.000	−0.010
Paraguay	0.213	0.189	0.130	0.001	0.008	0.017	−0.010	0.045	0.003	−0.008	0.005	0.000
Peru	0.439	0.334	0.267	0.000	0.002	0.007	0.007	0.145	−0.002	−0.011	0.000	−0.080
Uruguay	0.307	0.191	0.187	−0.005	−0.024	0.033	0.017	−0.004	0.006	−0.007	−0.003	−0.010
Venezuela, RB	0.049	−0.012	0.030	0.007	0.081	−0.005	−0.026	0.212	0.003	−0.022	0.000	−0.290
Mean	0.218	0.164	0.133	0.003	0.006	0.009	0.017	0.058	0.001	−0.008	0.002	−0.055

TABLE B.20: **Economic Growth Regressions**
(controlling for the output gap, GDP p.c. volatility, and RER volatility)

	Dependent variable: ln(GDP p.c.)	
	(1)	(2)
Variable	SYS GMM	LS
ln(GDP p.c.), $t-1$	0.64***	0.68***
	(0.06)	(0.05)
Output gap, $t-1$	1.66***	0.92***
	(0.33)	(0.26)
GDP p.c. volatility, t	−1.22**	0.15
	(0.56)	(0.44)
RER volatility, t	0.18	0.03
	(0.14)	(0.12)
Structural policies and institutions		
ln(secondary school enrollment rate), t	−0.09	−0.04
	(0.06)	(0.04)
ln(private domestic credit/GDP), t	0.04	0.03
	(0.03)	(0.02)
ln(structure adjusted trade volume/GDP), t	0.10*	0.10**
	(0.06)	(0.04)
ln(government consumption/GDP), t	−0.16**	−0.18***
	(0.07)	(0.05)
ln(telephone lines p.c.), t	0.18***	0.11***
	(0.03)	(0.03)
Polity2 score, t	−0.04	−0.02
	(0.04)	(0.02)
Stabilization policies		
Inflation rate, t	0.00	−0.01
	(0.01)	(0.01)
ln(real exchange rate), t	−0.11**	−0.03
	(0.05)	(0.04)
Banking crisis, t	−0.02	−0.05*
	(0.04)	(0.03)
External conditions		
ComPI growth, t	5.81**	6.01**
	(2.99)	(2.98)
Terms-of-trade growth, t	0.07**	0.08**
	(0.04)	(0.04)
AR (1) test, p-value	0.01	—

(continued on next page)

	(1)	(2)
	SYS GMM	LS
Variable		
AR (2) test, p-value	0.45	–
Country FE	Yes	Yes
Year FE	Yes	Yes
Observations	350	350
Countries	126	126

Dependent variable: ln(GDP p.c.)

Note: The dependent variable is real GDP per capita. The method of estimation in column (1) is system-GMM (system–general method of moments); column (2) is least squares. ComPI = international commodity export price index; FE = fixed effects; GDP = gross domestic product; LS = least squares; p.c. = per capita; RER = real exchange rate; SYS GMM = system–general method of moments; *t* = time.
*Significantly different from zero at the 10 percent significance level, ** 5 percent significance level, *** 1 percent significance level.

TABLE B.21: **Economic Growth Regressions**
(interaction model)

Dependent variable: ln(GDP p.c.)

Variable	(1) SYS GMM	(2) SYS GMM	(3) SYS GMM	(4) SYS GMM
Interaction variable	Inflation above median	Infrastructure above median	Financial development above median	Inflation below median, and infrastructure and financial development above median
	Panel A: Schooling			
ln(secondary school enrollment rate), t	0.07 (0.05)	0.06** (0.03)	0.06** (0.03)	0.05 (0.03)
ln(secondary school enrollment rate), t* interaction variable	−0.02 (0.02)	0.01 (0.01)	0.00 (0.01)	−0.02 (0.02)
Interaction variable	0.05 (0.08)	−0.01 (0.04)	0.01 (0.04)	0.12 (0.08)
ln(GDP p.c.), $t-1$	0.77*** (0.04)	0.80*** (0.04)	0.79*** (0.04)	0.79*** (0.04)
AR (1) test, p-value	0.00	0.00	0.00	0.00
AR (2) test, p-value	0.10	0.12	0.13	0.13
Sargan test, p-value	0.23	0.20	0.25	0.31
Country FE	Yes	Yes	Yes	Yes

(continued on next page)

	(1)	(2)	(3)	(4)
	Dependent variable: ln(GDP p.c.)			
Variable	SYS GMM	SYS GMM	SYS GMM	SYS GMM
Year FE	Yes	Yes	Yes	Yes
Observations	760	760	760	760
Countries	95	95	95	95
Panel B: Financial development				
ln(private domestic credit/GDP), t	0.09*** (0.04)	0.12*** (0.04)	–	0.11*** (0.03)
ln(private domestic credit/GDP), t * interaction variable	0.01 (0.01)	–0.02 (0.02)	–	–0.04 (0.01)
Interaction variable	–0.03 (0.05)	0.13** (0.06)	–	0.15*** (0.04)
ln(GDP p.c.), $t-1$	0.68*** (0.05)	0.65*** (0.05)	–	0.68*** (0.05)
AR (1) test, p-value	0.00	0.00	–	0.00
AR (2) test, p-value	0.00	0.00	–	0.01
Sargan test, p-value	0.36	0.30	–	0.45
Country FE	Yes	Yes	–	Yes
Year FE	Yes	Yes	–	Yes
Observations	800	800	–	800
Countries	100	100	–	100

Note: The dependent variable is real GDP per capita. The method of estimation is system-GMM (system–general method of moments). FE = fixed effects; GDP = gross domestic product; p.c. = per capita; SYS GMM = system–general method of moments; t = time.

*Significantly different from zero at the 10 percent significance level, ** 5 percent significance level, *** 1 percent significance level.

References

Arezki, R., and M. Brueckner. 2012. "Commodity Windfalls, Democracy, and External Debt." *Economic Journal* 122: 848–66.

Barro, R., and J. W. Lee. 2010. "A New Data Set of Educational Attainment in the World, 1950–2010." NBER Working Paper 15902, National Bureau of Economic Research, Cambridge, MA.

Dollar, David, and Aart Kraay. 2003. "Institutions, Trade, and Growth." *Journal of Monetary Economics* 50 (1): 133–62.

Feenstra, Robert C., Alan Heston, Marcel P. Timmer, and Haiyan Deng. 2009. "Estimating Real Production and Expenditures across Nations: A Proposal for Improving the Penn World Tables." *Review of Economics and Statistics* 91 (1): 201–212.

Reinhart, C., and K. Rogoff. 2011. "From Financial Crash to Debt Crisis." *American Economic Review* 101: 1676–1706.

World Bank. 2013. *World Development Indicators*. Online database. World Bank, Washington, DC. http://data.worldbank.org/indicator.